Strangers in the House

A Mysterious Comedy in Three Acts

By Victor Lucas

SEEVING THEATRE

S F

SINCE 1830

WWW.SAMUELFRENCH.CO.UK
WWW.SAMUELFRENCH.COM

ISBN 978-0-573-11202-7

www.samuelfrench.co.uk

www.samuelfrench.com

FOR AMATEUR PRODUCTION ENQUIRIES

UNITED KINGDOM AND WORLD
EXCLUDING NORTH AMERICA

plays@SamuelFrench-London.co.uk

020 7255 4302/01

Each title is subject to availability from Samuel French, depending upon country of performance.

PRODUCTION NOTES

If a wheelchair is not readily obtainable, the wheels and handle from a child's push-chair or perambulator can be utilised to convert an ordinary kitchen chair into a wheelchair suitable to the purposes of the play.

The old clothes worn by ARABELLA when masquerading as the Guy should be as ragged as possible, with straw protruding from the front of the jacket and from under the wide-brimmed slouch hat, so that the effect upon audiences of her unexpected sneeze will be really startling.

The " Thing " is a simple box-shaped object, placed on a small table and somewhat higher than a television set. It need be adorned only by a dial and a few knobs or it can be further embellished with red and green electric bulbs which light up when the " Thing " is switched on. It should be possible, with a very little inventive ingenuity, to give it a most amusing and intriguing face-like appearance . . indeed almost a robot personality of its own. An old tea chest, a little luminous paint, a few coloured bulbs should give the right result.

The off-stage fireworks in Act 3 should be as noisy as possible. In the interests of safety as well as simplicity, blank cartridges will provide the best effect.

The effect of the bonfire offstage just before the final curtain is best contrived by using an ordinary 1,000 watt flood fitted with a flame-coloured gelatine (5A) with patches of No. 6 Red stuck on here and there. A few strips of canvas about two feet long and 1½ inches wide are tacked to a short length of wood and suspended over the flood so that the strips hang down just in front of it. Move the strips to and fro and at the same time increase and decrease the light from the flood on the dimmer. The flickering effect on the walls of the room will provide an attractive picture as the curtain falls.

Pace is important to the play. MRS. BENBOW bowls all before her by the ripeness of her personality, though without, be it noted, losing her dignity or descending to mere aggressiveness. MRS. JONES is quite a gay, jolly woman and her husband conceals his absent-mindedness beneath a brisk manner.

Both PENNY and CYRIL are high-spirited young people; and JOHN CUNNINGHAM, despite the quietness of his charm, is a man of the world. A ponderous approach, slowness in delivering lines or picking up cues would handicap the play and are to be avoided at all costs. The PENNY and JOHN scenes can, of course, be taken at a slower pace than the rest of the play but should always be followed by an increase in tempo. This particularly applies after MR. JONES' entrance in Act Three, from which point there must be a general quickening of the pace and a feeling of mounting excitement right through to the end of the play, so that one revelation follows another in quick succession.

The cupboard door must have a handle on the outside which can be turned and rattled by CYRIL from within. Sundry old coats should be hanging inside the cupboard so that CYRIL is concealed when the door is opened.

The bolt on the main door must be a good solid metal one. The cigarette case used by CYRIL must be of the type which closes with an audible snap. Use a hanging chime for the grandfather clock, and the whistle from a whistling kettle for the percolator.

During the first interval tack gauze on the outside of the windows to give an appearance of fog but remove it during the second interval.

THE FURNITURE

There is a fairly large rectangular table L.C. and a small round one in front of the fireplace. Three chairs are set around the larger table.

Two armchairs, one above and one below the fire, at an angle.

A tall standard lamp behind the upstage armchair.

Radio above the fireplace.

Writing desk and chair U.L.

Sideboard above the kitchen door.

The " Thing " stands against the back wall, right of the archway.

A barometer hangs on the wall between the archway and the cupboard.

At the angle of the stairs is a heavy curtain and a fuse box visible to the audience.

In the hall, a telephone on a small table and also a coat stand.

The light switch is right of the cupboard.

WARDROBE

MRS. BENBOW Smart tailored costume. Pyjamas, dressing-gown, slippers.

MRS. JONES Bright woollen dress.

PENNY Skirt and trim sweater. Attractive pyjamas, dressing-gown, slippers.

ARABELLA As the Guy Fawkes; man's ragged clothing, black slouch hat, old grey woollen gloves and socks. (No shoes). Guy Fawkes mask. As herself; blue jeans and shapeless jumper beneath not very good coat. Ankle socks and pumps.

MISS FAIRFAX Glamorous and very smart costume. Spare pair of PENNY's pyjamas and dressing-gown.

MISS CHAMBERS Dark raincoat, black nylons, black gloves.

MR. JONES Lounge suit. Slippers.

CYRIL Lounge suit. Slippers. Flamboyant dressing-gown.

JOHN Well-cut grey flannels. Tweed jacket. Spare pair of Mr. Jones' pyjamas.

Outdoor coats, hats and gloves are worn by all characters at the appropriate times.

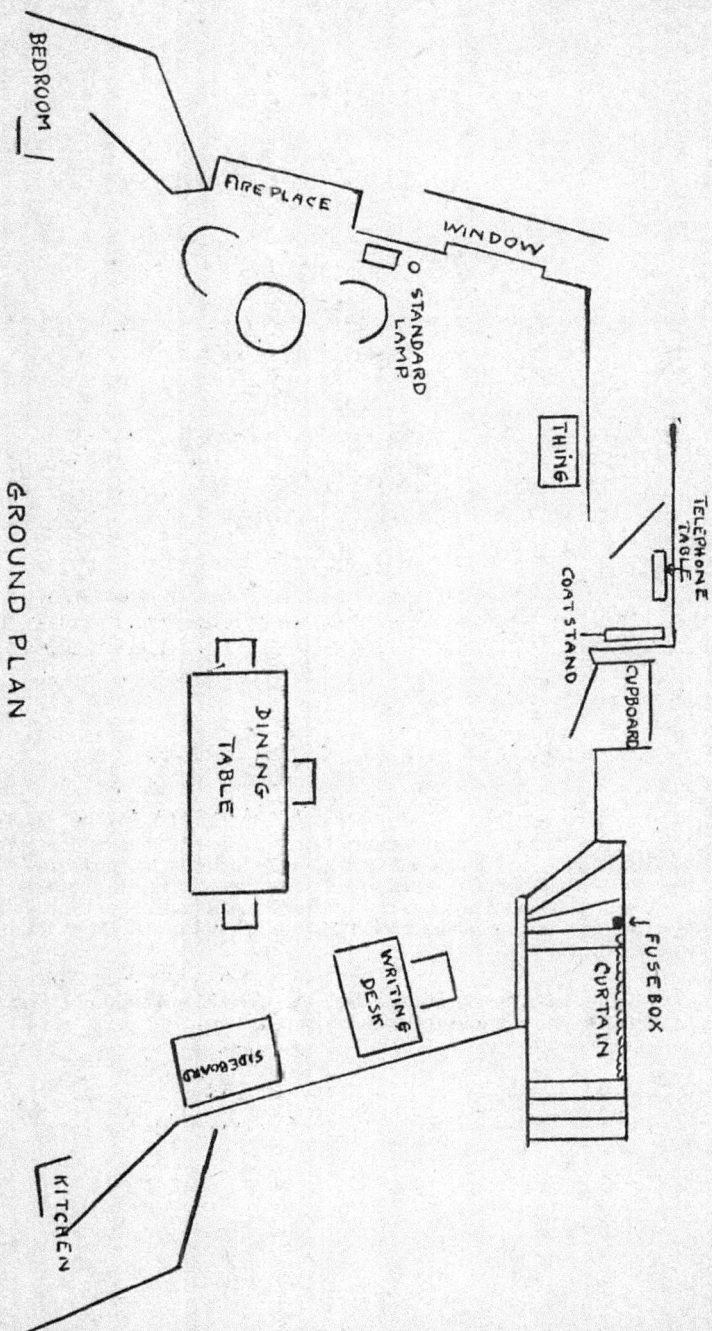

GROUND PLAN

BEDROOM

FIREPLACE

WINDOW

STANDARD LAMP

THING

TELEPHONE TABLE

COAT STAND

CUPBOARD

DINING TABLE

WRITING DESK

SIDEBOARD

FUSE BOX

CURTAIN

KITCHEN

CHARACTERS
(in the order of their appearance)

MRS. BENBOW

MRS. JONES

MR. JONES

PENNY JONES

CYRIL JONES

MISS CHAMBERS

MISS FAIRFAX

JOHN CUNNINGHAM

ARABELLA BUNTER-CUTTS

THE SCENE: The pleasantly furnished living-room of a suburban house. Down right is a door leading to CYRIL'S bedroom. Above this the fireplace and then tall windows which open on to the garden. In the Back Wall, right of centre, is an archway which leads to the hall and to the main door. Left of centre is a large cupboard. Left of this the staircase. Down left is a door to the kitchen.

Production notes, a stage plan, a property list, a wardrobe plot and details of the furniture are in the book of the play.

Strangers in the House

ACT ONE

(*When the curtain rises it is early evening on a Saturday in November. There is a cosy glow from the wall-brackets, the standard lamp and the fire. Gay music is playing softly on the radio. The general atmosphere is one of comfort and warmth.*
MRS. BENBOW *is in the armchair above the fire, smoking a cheroot and reading a book. She is a distinguished-looking woman in her early fifties.* MRS. JONES, *a pleasant motherly woman sits at the writing desk, chewing the end of her pen thoughtfully. Seized with sudden inspiration, she starts to write.* MR. JONES, *a retired Civil Servant, sits in the other armchair, completely engrossed with sundry pieces of wire and metal spread on the small table before him. His manner is absent-minded but at times deceptively brisk. He is wearing bedroom slippers.* PENNY JONES, *their daughter, comes quickly down the stairs, humming gaily. She wears an attractive dressing gown and carries several small bottles of nail varnish. In her last year as a teenager, she is a delightful person with great charm and a horse-tail hair style.*)

PENNY   Good evening Mrs. Benbow. (*She places the bottles on the large table.*)

MRS. BENBOW (*without looking up*)   Good evening, Penny.

PENNY   What are you reading? Something interesting?

MRS. BENBOW   El Akram yah Mookroosh.

PENNY   Pardon? (*She crosses to her.*)

MRS. BENBOW   It's "The Cocktail Party" translated into Arabic.

PENNY (*peering over the back of the armchair*)   Goodness! I think you're ever so clever to be able to read all those wiggles and squiggles.
(*She hurries blithely up the stairs on the end of her line and cannons into* CYRIL JONES *coming down in a state of agitation.*
CYRIL *is an amiable though somewhat fatuous young man. He descends the stairs in a hurry, performing a difficult feat by putting on his jacket and at the same time holding a handkerchief to his chin. He, too, is wearing slippers.*)

CYRIL (*in distress*)   Where's the sticking plaster! Has anyone seen the surgical spirit?

MRS. JONES   Cyril! (*She rises and moves to the sideboard*) I'll get the first-aid box. What have you been doing to yourself!

CYRIL   I'm scarred for life. It would happen tonight of all nights.

3

This is the last time I borrow Father's cut-throat.

MRS. JONES *(moving to him with a small first-aid box from the sideboard cupboard)* Sit down and let me see what you've done.

CYRIL *(taking the box from her)* Thank you, Mother. It's all right. Don't fuss. I can manage.

(He exits up the stairs and once again cannons into PENNY who is coming down. PENNY carries a newspaper which she spreads on the table.)

MRS. JONES Hurry up, Reg. We must get ready to go soon.

MR. JONES *(without looking up)* Yes . . . all right dear.

PENNY Are you going out too, Mother?

MRS. JONES *(crossing back to the writing desk and sitting)* Your father and I are having dinner with Mrs. Bunter-Cutts.

MRS. BENBOW *(looking up suddenly)* Bunter-Cutts? Bunter-Cutts? Who is this Mrs. Bunter-Cutts?

MRS. JONES She's the President of the League.

MRS. BENBOW Which League?

MRS. JONES The West Wimbledon Women's League of Self-Sufficiency.

MRS. BENBOW *(putting aside her book)* Tell me about this West Women's Wimbledon Whatever-it-was.

MRS. JONES It's a sort of club really. We organise outings and discussion groups and hold monthly meetings. Last month we had Richard Fulton from " Mrs. Dale's Diary " as our guest of honour. Such a charming man. Mrs. Bunter-Cutts is hoping to get Jonathan Gabriel next time.

PENNY *(interested)* Is she really! That *would* be something!

MRS. BENBOW Who's he?

MRS. JONES He writes every week in " Woman's Own."

PENNY *(staring into space)* I wonder what he looks like?

MRS. JONES I don't know. I don't think they've ever published a photograph of him.

PENNY He writes such lovely stories. *(She proceeds to paint her nails)* I'm sure he's tall and smouldering. Rather like Valentine Dyall.

MRS. BENBOW Nonsense. He's probably a decrepit old roué with eyes like oysters. I can just see him . . .

(CYRIL enters briskly down the stairs. He is straightening his tie, humming a tune and smoking a cigarette.)

. . . chain smoking as he ogles typists in Lower Regent Street.

CYRIL Talking about me?

MRS. JONES We were discussing Jonathan Gabriel.

CYRIL Never heard of him.

PENNY Oh Cyril, you must have done! He's famous! He writes all the Millicent books.

CYRIL What are *they?*

PENNY " Millicent Goes to School " . . . " Millicent and Tony " . . . " Millicent the Girl " . . .

4

MRS. JONES "Millicent the Wife" . . . "Millicent the Woman"
. . . "Millicent the Mother" . . .
(There is a brief pause while they search their memories.)
PENNY "Millicent's Gay Adventure" . . .
CYRIL *(brightening)* Ah! That sounds more my type of book!
PENNY *(picking up a novel with a gay cover from the sideboard)* I've
got one of his from the library now.
CYRIL *(taking it from her and moving away U.R.)* "Love Among
The Scented Blossoms" . . Any pictures?
PENNY Oh, he's a wonderful writer!
CYRIL *(reading from inside the front cover)* "Jonathan Gabriel
impales the heart of woman on the sharp thorns of his passionate
insight."
*(He chortles irreverently. PENNY snatches the book back from
him.)*
PENNY *(with dignity)* You couldn't be expected to understand.
CYRIL *(looking over MRS. BENBOW'S shoulder at the book she is
reading)* And what's Mrs. Benbow reading? Imbibing the
wisdom of the East, eh Mrs. Benbow? You'll be taking up
Yogi one of these days.
(To PENNY as he crosses above the table to D.L.)
I'll bet Jonathan Gabriel's a woman really. Real name Wilhelmina
Twitch. *(He exits D.L.)*
MRS. BENBOW It so happens I practised Yogi for many years when
I lived in a cave in the Atlas Mountains.
*(During the following dialogue MRS. JONES is sitting at the writing
desk U.L., alternately writing and thinking hard.)*
PENNY That's in North Africa isn't it?
MRS. BENBOW I'm surprised to find you so knowledgeable in
matters geographical.
PENNY It comes from working in a travel agency. You do get to
know the world, even if it is only at second hand. Venice . . .
Pernambuco . . . The Marquesas Islands . . . One day I want to
see all those places. One day I will.
MRS. BENBOW *(observing her shrewdly)* I had no idea you were
such a romantic.
PENNY *(coming back to the suburbs and busying herself with her nail
varnish)* What on earth were you doing in North Africa?
*(CYRIL enters D.L. and crosses rapidly behind the table to the
stairs.)*
MRS. BENBOW Observing the habits of the natives. Through
Yogi I attained to the fourth of the seven planes of dynamic
insight. But I gave it up on returning to England.
CYRIL *(pausing on the stairs)* Oh? Why?
MRS. BENBOW *(turning in her chair to address the remark to CYRIL)*
I found the contemplation of my navel an overrated pastime,
unsuited to the English climate.
CYRIL Oh. *(He exits up the stairs.)*

5

MRS. BENBOW Though still of course a convenient mental relaxation in the London Tube during the Rush Hour.

MRS. JONES How does this sound? " Use SPLOSHO and you soon will find your dishes sparkling and your cares behind." *(Doubtfully)* Not quite right is it?

(CYRIL enters down the stairs and crosses to his room D.R.)

PENNY I think Flaming June is just as seductive as Bleeding Heart. *(She extends a hand to CYRIL as he passes)* What do you think Cyril?

CYRIL Don't ask me. Ugh! They look like vampire's talons. *(He exits D.R.)*

MRS. JONES Personally I never use SPLOSHO for washing up. I did try it once but it took the skin off my hands and turned the knives and forks green.

MRS. BENBOW May I ask then, why you are extolling its virtues in rhyme?

MRS. JONES It's a competition, Mrs. Benbow. Find a rhyme and win five hundred pounds. Second prize—free admission for life to the Battersea Fun Fair and Pleasure Gardens."

MRS. BENBWO Good Grief!

MRS. JONES " A Thousand Consolation prizes of Giant Monster packets of SPLOSHO." Here's another one I've thought up.

(CYRIL enters D.R. with a pair of shoes in his hand and crosses towards the kitchen door D.L.)

" SPLOSHO'S the stuff for doing your chores. It washes down walls . . .

CYRIL *(pausing at the door D.L. for a moment)* And burns holes in the floors. *(He exits D.L.)*

MRS. BENBOW How long have you been doing these competitions Mrs. Jones?

MRS. JONES *(sighing)* Nearly twenty years.

PENNY And you've never won a thing. You must have spent pounds and pounds on stamps alone. Surely there are easier ways of tempting fortune.

(CYRIL enters D.L. with shoes, shoe-cleaning materials and a newspaper which he spreads on the table (left end).)

What with your competitions and Father's inventions . . . Hey, steady on there!

MRS. JONES Cyril! I do wish you'd clean your shoes in the kitchen. I'm tired of telling you!

CYRIL That's all right Mother. I shan't be a minute. Penny's the one who's cluttering up the table. *(He pushes her bottles further along, knocking over some which are fortunately corked.)*

PENNY Mind my Flaming June!

CYRIL *(reading from the newspaper)* " A box of fireworks with a fuse attached has been discovered beneath the Speaker's Chair in the House of Commons. This threat to explode the seat of Government . . ."

6

(MRS. BENBOW *rises suddenly.* CYRIL *stops and looks up.*)

MRS. BENBOW I must go. *(She exits up the stairs.)*

MRS. JONES *(doubtfully)* " SPLOSHO splashes well your dishes answers all your washing-up wishes."

CYRIL *(polishing)* I can't think why somebody didn't blow it up years ago.

MR. JONES *(without looking up)* What's that, son?

CYRIL The seat of Government.

MR. JONES *(his thoughts elsewhere)* I don't know. You'd better ask your mother. She knows where everything's kept in this house. I don't.

PENNY There. That ought to do for Mr. Prendergast.

MRS. JONES Penny, dear. How many girls has Mr. Prendergast working for him?

PENNY Well, there's Hilda and Miss Hibbert at the enquiry desk, there's young Janet who does the post and staves off the office boy and makes the tea . . . and then there's me in the private office.

MRS. JONES *(doubtfully)* With Mr. Prendergast.

PENNY What's on your mind, Mother?

MRS. JONES Didn't you tell me Mr. Prendergast was married?

PENNY That's right. He's separated from his wife though. He says she didn't understand him. I bet she did. It isn't difficult to understand Mr. Prendergast.

MRS. JONES You mustn't mind my asking, dear, but what exactly are his motives in taking you out tonight?

PENNY *(amused)* His motives? Oh, Mother, you are naive. *(She rises.)*

MRS. JONES Your father and I are concerned for you, dear. We don't want you to come to any harm.

PENNY *(hugging her)* Darling . . . what sheltered lives girls lived in your young days.

MRS. JONES Did we? Ah well, that's what we like you to think anyway.

(Offstage, a Grandfather Clock chimes five times with unnatural rapidity.)

(CYRIL, meanwhile, crosses quickly to the mantelpiece and picks up his wrist-watch. On putting it to his ear he finds that it has stopped.)

CYRIL *(as the last stroke dies away)* Anybody got the right time?

PENNY *(glancing at her watch)* Nearly ten to seven.

CYRIL *(strapping on his watch and adjusting it)* I do wish you hadn't mended all the clocks, Father. They were all right until you overhauled their pinwheels.

PENNY Can't they ever be put right again?

MR. JONES I've tried shortening the swing . . .

(Offstage a single chime from the Grandfather Clock.)

. . . but the trouble seems to lie with the ratchet.

7

(Offstage a belated double chime.)

CYRIL It's impossible to tell the time in this house nowadays with the clocks chiming all the wrong hours. *(He parts the hanging curtains at the window U.R. and peers out into the night.)*

MRS. JONES This sounds a nice one. First prize a week-end with Wilfred Pickles.

PENNY What's this? More SPLOSHO?

MRS. JONES No, this is for the best suggestion for what to do with BIKIWIX Breakfast Flakes.

(CRYIL taps the barometer.)

PENNY You're not trying to tell the time by that now are you? What's the matter with Cyril? Why are you on hot bricks?

CYRIL Never you mind.

(He sits left of the table and resumes polishing his shoes. MRS. BENBOW comes down the stairs. She now wears a coat and a hat.)

MRS. BENBOW *(majestically, as she moves to the street door)*

" Ah, would some power the giftie gie us

To see ourselves as others see us . . ."

(She exits to the accompaniment of blank looks from PENNY and CYRIL.

(MR. and MRS. JONES, quite engrossed, have taken no notice.)

PENNY Father, who exactly *is* Mrs. Benbow?

MR. JONES Mrs. Benbow? How do you mean?

PENNY She's been here three months and she's just as much an enigma now as she was on the day she arrived.

CYRIL Did you know she was going to be a permanent fixture when you first brought her home to supper?

MR. JONES *(mildly)* No. I merely wished to enjoy her conversation at greater length than was possible on a park bench. She's an interesting talker. Her views are usually worth listening to.

CYRIL And so Mother invites her to say the night . . .

PENNY And then she offers to put her up for the week . . .

CYRIL And she's been here ever since.

PENNY She can talk all right. When she wants to. But it seems to me that of late she's been behaving very oddly. Has she said anything about leaving?

MRS. JONES *(suddenly)* No, she hasn't. And I don't intend to ask her. She may be a little eccentric at times but she's a very nice woman. We have the room and since she insists on paying handsomely for her keep she's very welcome to stay as long as she likes.

CYRIL Does she still spend all her time in the Reading Room of the British Museum?

MRS. JONES I believe so.

PENNY *(aghast)* Whatever does she go there for?

MRS. JONES I understand she's engaged on some form of research.

CYRIL She's gathering material for a book. She told me all about it one night.

8

PENNY   What kind of a book?

CYRIL   She says it's a survey of Man's dependence on Woman through the Ages.

PENNY *(impressed)*   Crumbs!

MR. JONES *(clearing his throat without looking up)*   There's a very good book on centipedes. I don't know if you've read it.
(They wait for further details but none are forthcoming. They exchange a glance.)

PENNY   No, Father. I don't think we have.

MR. JONES   Then there was another one I read some time ago . . . all about Guy Fawkes. Very interesting. The man who wrote it had a theory that Guy Fawkes was really Christopher Marlowe who was really Shakespeare.

CYRIL   What's happened to *our* Guy Fawkes?

MRS. JONES   Mrs. Benbow put it back in the cupboard.

PENNY   She said it made her hackles rise. What are hackles?

CYRIL *(moving to the cupboard)*   I don't think he should be locked away in a dark cupboard.

PENNY   Quite right.
(She joins CYRIL as he opens the cupboard.)
Let's bring him out.

CYRIL   After all, this time tomorrow he'll be sitting on top of our bonfire.

PENNY   Let him enjoy a little social life while he can.
(They proceed to wheel GUY FAWKES out of the cupboard.)

MRS. JONES   Where do the years go? It seems scarcely possible but we've used that old chair every November the Fifth for nearly twenty years now. Ever since Cyril was a boy of five. I can still remember the first Guy Fawkes you ever made for him.

MR. JONES   I remember. That was the time Cyril had the measles.
(CYRIL places GUY FAWKES, in his chair, against the back wall left of the archway.)

CYRIL   I'll say this Father. You may not be the world's best clock-mender but your guys get more lifelike every year.
(The telephone rings.)

PENNY *(moving towards the phone)*   I'll get it.

CYRIL *(forestalling her)*   No you won't, little sister. It's for me.

PENNY   Hey! How do you know? Who is it?

CYRIL *(at telephone)*   Hello? . . . Darling! Mmm! Sweetheart! How's my woman of mystery?

PENNY   Suffering cats! *(She sits R. of the table.)*

CYRIL   Darling, that's sweet of you . . . Darling, you have the most wonderful inspirations . . . All right, Honeypot.
(PENNY makes a noise indicating acute nausea.)

CYRIL   I shall have to hang up now, darling. There's a small child here making a noise. Same place . . . same time. 'Bye darling.

9

(He hangs up and catches PENNY'S *eye upon him.)*
What are you staring at?

PENNY   Who is this woman of mystery . . . this pot of honey?

CYRIL   Is there no privacy in this house?   *(He collects his overcoat and scarf from the stand in the hall.)*

PENNY   What's old Cyril up to?   Who was at the other end of that phone, Mother?   Anyone I know?

MRS. JONES   I don't suppose so dear.
*(*CYRIL *comes back into the room carrying overcoat and scarf. Gloves are in the overcoat pockets.   He puts coat and scarf over chair left of table and proceeds to change from slippers to shoes.)*

PENNY   He's a gay young spark is our Cyril.   I wonder if he's wallowing in some delicious intrigue.   Where are you off to tonight?

CYRIL   To lands of pagan enchantment . . to eat lotus buds in the shade of the bong tree.   Mind your own business.

PENNY   Are you having an affaire with her?

MRS. JONES   Ssh!   Penny!

PENNY   Personally I'm all for it.   It might do Cyril a lot of good. He needs a woman's admiration to bolster up his ego.

MRS. JONES   Penny!   I don't think that's a very nice thing to say.

PENNY   Why not?   I think we should all throw off the shackles of convention and live life to the full.

MRS. JONES   Stop dramatising yourself, Penny.

PENNY *(dramatically)*   Why is there one law for the man and another for the woman?   I must look around and find a rich protector.

MRS. JONES   Penny!

CYRIL *(chuckling)*   You read too many novels.

PENNY   Why don't we know any artists?   I rather like the thought of passion in a mews in Chelsea.

CYRIL   You'll end up with rheumatism and a bearded surrealist in a damp basement off Hammersmith Broadway.

PENNY   I think it's a lovely idea.

CYRIL   Rheumatism in a basement?

PENNY   No . . . passion in a mews.

MRS. JONES   There's more to marriage than you seem to think dear.

PENNY   Marriage?   That's for the timid and unadventurous.

MRS. JONES   Nonsense dear.   Absolute nonsense.

PENNY   Well anyway, it's an out-dated arrangement.   *(She gathers together her bottles, etc.)*

CYRIL   Only nineteen and listen to her.   What's she going to be like when she's thirty?

MRS. JONES   She'll fall in love long before then and settle down like everybody else.

PENNY   Ah, love!   *(She rises)*   Love is the bloom on the crimson petals of passion.   *(She moves to the foot of the stairs.)*

10

MRS. JONES Penny! Really! That's quite enough. You'll scandalize your father.

MR. JONES *(looking up)* What's that dear?

MRS. JONES Nothing, Reg. Just you carry on with what you're doing.
(PENNY starts to go upstairs.)
Just a moment Penny. Where is it you're going with Mr. Prendergast?

PENNY Don't worry, Mother. I'm a big girl now. I can look after myself.

MRS. JONES I wonder.

PENNY He's got tickets for the new British Musical at Drury Lane. I believe it's ever so good.

MRS. JONES Oh yes . . . what's it called?

PENNY " Dames and Guys." It's all about American Marines in Stoke-on-Trent. *(She sits.)*

MRS. JONES *(putting her papers away)* Oh well, I suppose times change and we must change with them. Come along Reg, put that away. I said we'd be there for dinner at eight o'clock. *(She exits up the stairs.)*

CYRIL *(putting on his coat and scarf)* What is it you're making Father? Another of your inventions, is it?

MR. JONES Mmm . . . ? Oh . . . it's just an idea I had. It's a sort of silencer. A little gadget you could fix inside a tank.

CYRIL A tank! *(He whistles)* Gosh! Are you going to send it to the War Office? If they're interested there might be quite a bit of money in it.

MR. JONES The War Office? Oh, no, I don't think so. My idea was . . . to fix it inside the tank in the W.C.

CYRIL Oh . . . really, Father! Whatever for?

MR. JONES To stop the cistern singing. You know what a noise it makes in the middle of the night.

CYRIL I can't make up my mind whether my father's a genius or just a jack of all trades. Since you returned you've invented a dozen or more gadgets and have any of them ever worked? Not one.

MR. JONES Oh well, of course . . .

CYRIL There was that device for the speedier peeling of shrimps . . . .

MR. JONES That very nearly . . .

CYRIL I remember your super-swift sock-darning attachment to a sewing machine.

MR. JONES It almost . . .

CYRIL And of course, there's always . . . the THING. *(He indicates the sheet-shrouded object U.R.C.)*
(PENNY enters down the stairs, dressed and wearing a smart coat.)
Father, the time has come for you to be frank. I want a straight answer to a straight question. What *is* the THING?

11

MR. JONES *(evasively)* Oh . . its just an idea I had.

PENNY Yes, we know that. For months you scoured the junk shops and came home every day with pulleys, springs . . .

CYRIL Coils of wire . . . the remains of an old mowing machine . . .

PENNY And half the inside of a motor car. Then came the weeks of hammering and banging in the woodshed . . .

CYRIL But now that it's finished, roped and wrapped and set in a place of honour in the living room . . . *what is it!!! (He whisks away the sheet.)*
Is it a fruit machine . . . a juke box . . . Robbie the Robot . . . a home-made television set?

MR. JONES No, it isn't. No.

(MRS. JONES enters down the stairs, wearing coat and hat ready to go out.)

CYRIL Father's still being maddeningly evasive about the THING. Do you know what it's for?

MRS. JONES If your father doesn't want to talk about it you must wait until he's ready. *(She replaces the sheet.)* Hurry up Reg or we shall be late.

MR. JONES I'll just go and wash my hands . . . put on a clean collar . . . *(He exits up the stairs.)*

PENNY Was Father always like this?

MRS. JONES Like what?

PENNY Just the least little bit crackers.

MRS. JONES Don't exaggerate. He's simply absent-minded, that's all. *(She exits D.L.)*

CYRIL Now we're alone I want a word with you, young Penelope. How far has this business gone?

PENNY Which business? What are you blathering about?

CYRIL This Prendergast business; you'd better watch your step young woman.

PENNY *I* had? Why?

CYRIL Sooner or later your Mr. Prendergast will want to know which side his bread's buttered.

PENNY If you mean what I think you mean you've got a nasty mind. I can handle Prendy. Besides I like him. He's sweet.

CYRIL Sweet, is he?

PENNY He's round and chubby like a big cuddly bear.

CYRIL Do you think it's quite the thing to do?

PENNY What?

CYRIL Why, to run around all over the place with a middle-aged and heavily married cuddly bear.

PENNY Oh pooh.

CYRIL There are plenty of eligible young bachelors ready and willing to compete for your favours, given a little encouragement.

PENNY I know. I've met them at dances. Covered in spots and not yet come to man's estate. I'm bored with young bachelors. They don't understand women . . . not one little bit. They're just beginners, groping in the dark.

CYRIL   Groping in the . . . !

PENNY   You poke your nose into your own affairs. Leave me to manage mine.

CYRIL   That's all very well, but what's his wife going to say about it?

PENNY   I've told you he's separated from his wife.

CYRIL   But don't you realise this may be what she's been waiting for?

PENNY   What do you mean?

CYRIL   I'm all for youth having its fling and all that sort of thing. But I don't want to see my only begotten sister cited as co-respondent in a divorce case.
(MR. JONES *comes down the stairs minus coat and collar and still wearing slippers.)*
Father, I think you ought to put your foot down.
(MR. JONES *looks mystified and goes to the small table by the fire to collect his paraphanalia.)*
Penny's too young to have Queen's Proctors on her tail.

PENNY   Queen's Proctors? What on earth are *they?*

CYRIL   You're old enough to know better.

PENNY   First I'm too young and then I'm too old. Which is it? I wish you'd make up your mind. Queen's Proctors indeed!

MR. JONES   Chipping Priors is a very pretty little place too. There's an old Saxon church, a seventeenth century inn . . the best rough cider in the Cotswolds . . *(He exits D.L.)*
(CYRIL *and* PENNY *stare after him for a second and then both burst into laughter.)*

PENNY   The old man's really going round the bend!

CYRIL   *(more reasonably than before)* Look . . . about this Prendergast business . . .

PENNY   Now Cyril, I don't want to hear . . .

CYRIL   No, wait a minute. I don't wish to pry. I am not myself beyond reproach.

PENNY   *(affectionately)* Oh Cyril, you are a clot!

CYRIL   He that casts the first stone should take the beam out of his own eye . . or whatever it is . . but all the same . . .

PENNY   *(linking her arm with his)* Cyril, it's very nice of you to try to protect me from the big bad wolves of this world. But, believe me, I'm not exactly Red Riding Hood.

CYRIL   It's just that I'm fond of my little sister. I mean, after all, blood's stronger than water . . . and thicker too.
(MR. JONES *enters D.L. carrying a pair of well-polished shoes.)*

MR. JONES   Hello, you two. You're back early. Did you have a good time? Don't touch that, will you. *(He indicates the* THING*)* It may blow up. *'He exits up the stairs.)*

PENNY   This is getting really serious! He lives in a world of his own.

13

CYRIL It's this . . this . . THING. It's become an obsession with him.

PENNY You're right. It's like some sort of a robot . . . a Frankenstein. *(She stares thoughtfully at the* THING.*)*

CYRIL Forty years of sober efficiency as the most civil of Civil Servants and then the moment he retires he becomes the complete absent-minded professor. Half the time he doesn't even hear what you say to him.

PENNY Has it ever struck you that Mrs. Benbow and Father are two of a feather?

CYRIL How do you mean?

PENNY Did you know they get up in the middle of the night and hold long conversations down here in whispers?

CYRIL Do they?

PENNY It's a fact. I often hear the floorboards creak as Mrs. Benbow pads downstairs in her stockings. Last night I watched them from the top of the stairs.

CYRIL What were they talking about?

PENNY I couldn't catch what they were saying but . . . it was something to do with the THING!

CYRIL How do you know?

PENNY First they unwrapped part of it and then they kept tapping it and looking inside it. Mrs. Benbow took this white sheet and draped it around herself. She looked ever so spooky with the lights out and the moon shining in through the window.

CYRIL Why should she do that?

PENNY Search me.

CYRIL *(after a pause)* Perhaps they were playing Druids.

PENNY I've just thought. It all ties up with that other business.

CYRIL You mean that girl who was watching the house?

PENNY Not only that. Something very odd happened yesterday.

CYRIL What?

PENNY I came home earlier than usual and as I turned the corner I saw two foreign-looking men come out of the house. They got into a big Rolls-Royce and drove away.

CYRIL Who were they?

PENNY I don't know. When I came in, Father was standing by the THING, staring at it with a very odd look on his face. He put the sheet back as soon as he saw me.

CYRIL Did he say anything?

PENNY I asked him who the men were but he was in one of his facetious moods and said something about them calling to read the gas meter. He seemed strangely excited about something.

CYRIL Where does Mrs. Benbow fit into all this?

PENNY I don't know yet. *(She turns suddenly)* Cyril . . what do we actually know about her?

CYRIL Very little, apart from the fact that she's knocked about the world a bit and smokes cigars. Why?

PENNY *(thoughtfully)* She never has any letters does she? Nobody ever calls to see her or rings her up.
CYRIL She had a phone call today.
PENNY When?
CYRIL Just after tea. While you were having your bath.
PENNY What was it about?
CYRIL I don't know but I heard her say " All right. If *you* can't make it, I'll have to get hold of her." Then she hung up.
PENNY Interesting. I asked her once if there was a *Mr.* Benbow.
CYRIL What did she say?
PENNY She said, " I have no living relatives. Neither kith nor kin nor encumberances. I walk alone."
(Offstage the Grandfather Clock chimes once.)
CYRIL There's something very odd about her.
PENNY You don't think she's hiding from the police, do you?
CYRIL Eh?
PENNY If the police were after her the last thing she'd do would be to stay at a hotel, where she could be traced. This is the perfect hide-out!
CYRIL You're right. The whole street fairly reeks of respectability.
PENNY I wonder what she could have done? Let's see . . there's forgery, burglary, bigamy, smuggling . . . Smuggling! That could be it! It all adds up; Mrs. Benbow, the two foreigners in the big car, the girl who was watching the house. But where does Father come in?
(Offstage two more chimes.)
CYRIL There's that lying pendulum again. *(He glances at his watch.)* Ten past seven. Are you going to the bus stop?
PENNY Yes.
CYRIL We'll talk this over as we go. There's something going on in this house that we're not supposed to know about.
PENNY Do you know what I think?
CYRIL What?
(The Kitchen Door D.L. opens slowly.)
PENNY Ssh! Look out. I'll tell you later.
(MRS. JONES enters D.L.)
We're off now, Mother.
MRS. JONES Enjoy yourselves.
CYRIL Goodnight, Mother.
MRS. JONES Don't be late.
(CYRIL and PENNY exit C.)
(MRS. JONES collects empty coffee cups from small table by fire and exits with them into the kitchen D.L.)
(MR. JONES enters down the stairs, now wearing shoes but still minus collar and tie which protrude from a pocket of the jacket carried over his arm. He holds in his hand a screwdriver. He puts his jacket on the right end of the large table. Humming a

tuneless tune, he partly folds back the sheet and proceeds to make minor adjustments to the back of the THING.)

*(*MRS. JONES *enters D.L.)*

MRS. JONES   I thought you were upstairs getting ready. This is no time to tinker with the THING.

MR. JONES   What is it we're going to see?

MRS. JONES   Oh really!

MR. JONES   You did tell me, I know, but I've forgotten. I hope it's better than that last film we went to.

MRS. JONES   We're not going to the cinema.

MR. JONES   We're not?

MRS. JONES   *(picking up his jacket from the large table)*   We're dining with the Bunter-Cutts. I told you. Nobody ever listens to anything I say.

MR. JONES   Yes we do.

MRS. JONES   You simply take me for granted and so do the children. I suppose it's only natural. But sometimes I wonder how little it would mean to any of you if I were to fade quietly out of your lives. I doubt if you'd even notice I'd gone. Would you?

MR. JONES   That'll do it. I thought I'd better disconnect it before we went out. I wouldn't want Cyril to meddle with it and blow us all up. It's the sort of thing he would do. He's very irresponsible, you know. I've often noticed that. Half the time he doesn't seem to hear what one says to him.

*(*MRS. JONES, *a tolerant smile on her lips, helps him into his jacket.)*

MRS. JONES   Look at you. Covered in fluff. *(She hands him his collar and tie)*   Put these on while I get the clothes brush. *(She goes to the coat stand U.C.)*

MR. JONES   Did you say the Bunter-Cutts? I remember them. Wasn't that where we went to see that play on television?

MRS. JONES   That's right. *(She comes down with the brush and starts to brush his suit.)*

MR. JONES   Who was that woman they had staying with them?

MRS. JONES   Which woman?

MR. JONES   A domineering woman with a glint in her eye and a tendency towards standing up and making speeches.

MRS. JONES   *That* was Mrs. Bunter-Cutts.

MR. JONES   Oh. Was it? Well I didn't care for her. She never stopped asking me questions.

MRS. JONES   What sort of questions?

MR. JONES   First she wanted to know my views on reincarnation and then she asked me how old you were.

MRS. JONES   *(handing him his overcoat and scarf)*   And what did you say?

MR. JONES   I damn nearly told her to mind her own business. I contented myself with remarking that my wife's age had always been a mystery to me.

16

*(*MRS. JONES *laughs and helps him on with his overcoat.)*
That woman's a menace. She'd ferret out the secrets of the
Sphinx.

MRS. JONES She is well-informed certainly.

MR. JONES Well-informed! She's a walking oracle on matters
that don't concern her. She asked me things about you and the
neighbours it had never occurred to me to consider.

MRS. JONES Here's your hat. I do believe you're ready at last.

MR. JONES Thank you Maud. *(He kisses her absent-mindedly)*
The things she told me about the private life of Tom Riley the
Town Clerk are not only untrue but physically impossible at his
age.

MRS. JONES You musn't take her too seriously.

MR. JONES Why are we going to the Bunter-Cutts? Can't we go
somewhere else?

MRS. JONES *(straightening the sheet)* Of course we can't. They're
expecting us.

MR. JONES I can understand them expecting *you*. But what am
I going there for?

MRS. JONES I asked you if you'd like to come and you said you
would.

MR. JONES I did? I don't remember that.

MRS. JONES Of course you did. Nearly a week ago. You can't
wriggle out of it at the last minute.

MR. JONES You've got me muddled now. I don't know whether
I'm coming or going.

MRS. JONES You're *going* and there's no more to be said. Come
along now. It will soon be eight o'clock. *(She switches off the
standard lamp.)*

MR. JONES I wish you'd tell me about these things beforehand.
I'm not at all keen on going to the Bunter-Cutts. We might
meet that woman there.

(They exit C., MRS. JONES switching off the main lights.)

(As they go the offstage Grandfather Clock chimes once.)

(There is a pause . . and then . . suddenly the GUY FAWKES *sneezes.
She—for the Guy Fawkes mask, old clothes and slouch hat conceal
the identity of* ARABELLA BUNTER-CUTTS—*gets out of her chair.
She examines the* THING *and then exits into* CYRIL'S *bedroom
D.R.)*

*(*MISS CHAMBERS *enters through the long window from the garden
U.R. She is a tall dark-haired woman in her early forties. Her
manner carries authority. She wears black gloves and carries a
torch which she flashes around the room. She cautiously makes
her way up the stairs and exits.)*

(The GUY FAWKES *enters from* CYRIL'S *bedroom and moves towards
the stairs.)*

*(*VOICES *are heard outside the door U.C.)*

(The GUY FAWKES *returns hurriedly to her chair.)*

17

*(*MRS. BENBOW *and* MISS FAIRFAX *enter U.C.* MISS FAIRFAX *is a smartly dressed and self-assured young woman of about twenty-five.)*

MISS FAIRFAX I feel like a burglar.

MRS. BENBOW. It's all right. You needn't whisper. *(She switches on the lights.)* The house is quite empty.

MISS FAIRFAX *(moving to behind the large table)* How are you getting along with your guinea pigs?

MRS. BENBOW They're interesting people. Very good-hearted. Eminently representative of their type. *(She picks up a briefcase from the right side of the upstage armchair.)*

MISS FAIRFAX Wasn't it a risk bringing me here tonight?

MRS. BENBOW Not at all. *(She crosses to the large table and unlocks the briefcase with a key from her coat pocket.)* I make a point of knowing their movements and habits, their comings-in and their goings-out. I know the routine of this household as well as I know the workings of their minds. *(She produces a long fat envelope from the briefcase.)* Take good care of this. There'll be more in due course.

MISS FAIRFAX Good. *(She takes the envelope and crosses to the fireplace.)*

MRS. BENBOW You can tell our friend that everything is proceeding according to plan. I'm even using the cat.

MISS FAIRFAX What's his name?

MRS. BENBOW Lucifer. A superior Persian with an arrogant air and a shameful fear of mice.

MISS FAIRFAX I didn't see the parents very clearly, but they looked nice people.

MRS. BENBOW They are. The salt of the earth.

MISS FAIRFAX What about the son and daughter?

MRS. BENBOW Absolutely right. She's frisky with a zest for life. He's an amiable though somewhat fatuous young man.

MISS FAIRFAX *(smiling)* I know the type. *(She turns away to extend her hands to the fire)*

*(*MRS. BENBOW *is left of the large table, locking the briefcase again.)* *(The* GUY FAWKES *gives vent to a suppressed sneeze, instinctively placing a finger beneath its nose and then hurriedly removing its hand to the arm of the chair again.)*

MRS. BENBOW Bless you.

(She and MISS FAIRFAX *turn at the same moment.)* What's the matter?

MISS FAIRFAX I must be going mad. For a moment I thought . . . *(She indicates the* GUY FAWKES.*)*

MRS. BENBOW Very lifelike, isn't it? The father made it.

MISS FAIRFAX It gives me the creeps.

MRS. BENBOW Me too. I'll put it back in the cupboard. *(She proceeds to do so.)* It's extraordinary how supposedly civilised beings will seize an opportunity to revive that most pagan of customs . . . the burning of the effigy. There is a close link between this and the idol cults, the voodoo and the devil worship practised by the primitive tribes of the Lower Zambezi. There. *(She closes the cupboard door.)*

MISS FAIRFAX *(now left of the* THING*)* And what's this? *(She starts to lift a corner of the sheet.)*

*(*MRS. BENBOW *forestalls her and replaces the sheet.)*

MRS. BENBOW Never mind about that. Come upstairs. There's something in my room I want you to see.

MISS FAIRFAX Suppose they come back unexpectedly?

MRS. BENBOW If they did, I should pass you off as my niece. But they won't. Not tonight. Come along. I want the benefit of your average woman's outlook.

MISS FAIRFAX Am I the average woman?

MRS. BENBOW Not you my dear. You're one of the special ones. A gallant flaming creature.

(She turns out the lights and they ascend the stairs together.)

But you have your finger on the feminine pulse. That's one of the reasons you're so useful to us.

(They exit. As they go the offstage Grandfather Clock starts to chime slowly and sonorously. The GUY FAWKES *emerges from the cupboard and creeps stealthily up the stairs. As it exits . . .*

THE CURTAIN FALLS

ACT TWO

(Later that evening. CYRIL is sitting in the upstage armchair, endeavouring to solve a crossword puzzle. The standard lamp above his chair is switched on, but the main lights are off. A military band can be heard playing on the radio.
(After a moment PENNY enters U.C.)

PENNY *(hanging up her coat)* Hullo. You're back early.

CYRIL *(switching off the radio)* So are you. I thought you were going to see " Dames and Guys."

PENNY *(switching on the main lights)* We were. But poor old Prendy's got a touch of flu. By the time we arrived at the theatre, his false teeth were chattering nineteen to the dozen.

CYRIL So what did you do?

PENNY When pain and anguish wrack the bones. A ministering angel Penny Jones.

CYRIL Are you sure you've got that right?

PENNY It's Mother's Splosho slogan complex coming out in me. There was only one thing to do and so I did it.

CYRIL What?

PENNY Took him back to his grass-widower's flat and put him to bed with a hot toddy. What about you? What's cut short your evening with the honey-pot?

CYRIL *(hedging)* What's a heavenly body in eight letters?

PENNY Never mind about your old crossword puzzle. What happened?

(CYRIL throws down his pencil.)

CYRIL Women are unpredictable . . . inexplicable.

(PENNY turns the chair right of the large table and sits astride it facing him.)

PENNY Well go on. I'm all ears and attention.

CYRIL They're odd creatures. I sometimes wonder if they think of anything but their own convenience.

PENNY You're growing up Cyril. The facts of life are dawning on you fast. What transpired?

CYRIL Nothing transpired. She wasn't there. She was before and so was he but not when I was. By the time I was she wasn't either and neither was he.

PENNY Dear old Cyril. You do make things crystal clear don't you. What on earth are you nattering about?

CYRIL *(patiently)* We arranged to meet in the Beehive. You know, at the corner of the High Street, opposite the Turkish Baths. That's where we first met nearly six weeks ago.

PENNY In the Turkish Bath?

CYRIL No, idiot girl, in the Beehive. I arrived on time but by then she'd been and gone. She left a note for me with the bar-maid. Here it is . . . *(He produces a sheet of paper from his*

20

pocket) " Sorry darling but duty calls unexpectedly. Ring me tomorrow. In haste. Elisabeth."

PENNY   Mmm! Sounds a bit fishy to me.

CYRIL   The odd thing is that according to Cynthia . . . she's the barmaid . . . a man came in tonight only five minutes before I arrived. He bought her a gin and then she went off with him.

PENNY   Who did . . . Cynthia?

CYRIL   Elisabeth. I don't know what to make of it.

PENNY   Oh well, if you will go picking up girls in pubs . . .

CYRIL   It wasn't in the pub. She was in the phone box outside.

PENNY   Fancy meeting in a phone box. Bit of a squash wasn't it?

CYRIL   I was passing. She only had a threepenny bit.

PENNY   Yes.

CYRIL   What do you mean by that remark?

PENNY   Now let's get this straight. This honey-pot picks you up for threepence outside the Beehive . . . Oh, that's rather good, isn't it? Beehive . . . honey-pot.

CYRIL   Very funny. Ha. Ha.

PENNY   Oh well, we all have to pay for our experience.

CYRIL   But it's not like her. We've been out a lot together and . . . well, she's not that kind of a girl.

PENNY   What kind of a girl is she? Come on, tell Auntie Penny. I can see you've taken this thing to heart.

CYRIL   *(warmly)* Oh, she's marvellous. She's beautiful. Tall, slender as an elm. When she walks I think of summer breezes rippling a field of corn.

PENNY   Hm. The slinky type. She sounds as if she spends all her working life lolling on leopard skins.

CYRIL   *(lyrically)* Her voice is like liquid music.

PENNY   You've got it bad. Thank heavens I'm a realist, not a woolly-minded romantic like you. You wouldn't catch me falling hook line and sinker for any man.

(The DOORBELL *rings. One abrupt fateful ring.)*

Who can that be?

CYRIL   It's somebody ringing our doorbell.

PENNY   *(rising)* No one can put two and two together as quickly as you can. *(She stops suddenly, facing the door.)* Oh . . !

CYRIL   What's the matter?

PENNY   *(turning slowly)* I've got a funny sort of warm feeling in my tummy.

CYRIL   It's those buttered shrimps we had for tea. I thought you ate yours too quickly.

PENNY   No fathead. A lovely sort of cosy feeling. Like knowing something is going to happen.

(The DOORBELL *rings again.)*

CYRIL   Well go on. Aren't you going to open it?

*(*PENNY *opens the door U.C.)*

JOHN   *(outside the door)* Oh. Good evening.

21

PENNY *(in a small voice)* Good evening.

JOHN I was looking for a Mrs. Benbow. I think perhaps I've mistaken the number. It's difficult to see in this fog.

PENNY No, you're quite right. Mrs. Benbow does live here. Won't you come in?

JOHN Thank you.

(He enters, removing his hat. He is a tall and good-looking man of thirty with a quiet charm.)

I didn't realise there'd be anyone else here tonight. Could you tell Mrs. Benbow I'm here.

PENNY As a matter of fact she's out.

JOHN Out!

PENNY This is my brother Cyril.

JOHN Are you sure?

PENNY Oh yes, I've known him for years.

JOHN *(turning to* CYRIL*)* How do you do. I meant are you *sure* she's out?

PENNY Yes, but you'd better stop because she'll be back quite soon.

CYRIL Will she? How do you know?

*(*PENNY *glares at* CYRIL *and then turns all her charm on* JOHN.*)*

PENNY Won't you sit down until she comes?

JOHN Well . . . I . . .

CYRIL Do you know Mrs. Benbow well?

JOHN *(guardedly)* Yes . . . and no.

PENNY Have you known her long or are you old friends?

*(*JOHN *looks nonplussed.)*

CYRIL She means did you know her before?

JOHN Before what?

CYRIL Before we did.

JOHN I shouldn't think so.

(There is an awkward pause.)

PENNY It's a small world isn't it?

CYRIL *(offering his case)* Have a cigarette.

JOHN *(taking one)* Thanks.

PENNY Do sit down.

(She picks up a box of matches from the table. JOHN *sits in the upstage armchair.)*

We're rather interested in Mrs. Benbow.

(She holds a lighted match for JOHN's *cigarette at the same moment that* CYRIL *offers his lighter.)*

JOHN *(regarding her over the lighted match)* Are you? *(He lights the cigarette)* Why?

PENNY Well, she seems rather *odd* sometimes.

JOHN *(glancing casually at* CYRIL's *crossword puzzle which is on the small table)* We're all rather odd *sometimes*.

PENNY We were wondering if . . .

JOHN Four down should be asteroid.

22

CYRIL   Which one is that?

JOHN   Heavenly body. Eight letters.

PENNY   What's an asteroid? Is it one of those little dots with points coming out of it?

JOHN *(smiling)* I'm afraid not. That's an asterisk. An asteroid is an undersized planet. Some of them are simply chunks of rock a few miles in diameter.

PENNY *(regarding him shrewdly)* How fascinating. Are there many of them?

JOHN   A tremendous number. So many that astronomers have run out of names to give them. There's even one called Marlene Deitrich.

PENNY   How clever you are. And awfully good at changing the subject too.

(JOHN bursts out laughing.)

JOHN   You're really determined to find out why I'm here, aren't you?

PENNY   Well, naturally we're curious.

JOHN   About Mrs. Benbow?

PENNY   About you too.

JOHN   Why? There's nothing especially odd or peculiar about me is there?

PENNY   Oh, but there is. *(Dramatically)* You walk into our lives out of the night .. shrouded in fog .. a complete stranger . . .

JOHN *(smiling)* My name is Cunningham. John Cunningham. I'm thirty years of age, my blood group is O2 and my business with Mrs. Benbow is of a private nature. Anything else?

PENNY   Are your married?

JOHN *(surprised)* No, I'm not. Why?

PENNY   I wondered. By the way, could you cope with a percolator?

JOHN   A what?

PENNY *(crossing to the kitchen D.L.)* I thought I'd make some coffee. The snag is our coffee percolator's one of the screw-up type and somebody's screwed it up too tight so we can't get the top off. I'm sure you have a lovely strong grip.

JOHN *(rising, amused)* Is the kitchen over there?

PENNY *(holding the door open for him to go through)* You're nice. So willing.

CYRIL   Can I help?

PENNY *(sternly)* You stay there and finish your crossword.

JOHN *(at the kitchen door)* Does she always order people about like this?

CYRIL   She is inclined to be a bit bossy.

PENNY   Take no notice of Cyril. He's rather in the dumps this evening.

JOHN   I'm sorry to hear that. Why?

23

PENNY He's had a hard day at the bank, shovelling up sixpenses in his little silver shovel.

(JOHN exits. PENNY beams happily at CYRIL and then follows JOHN into the kitchen. CYRIL goes into the hall and fills his cigarette case from a packet in his overcoat pocket. Whilst he is thus engaged MISS CHAMBERS peers round the top of the stairs. The room being apparently empty she hurries down intending to exit centre.)

(Just before she reaches the centre archway she hears CYRIL snap his case shut. MISS CHAMBERS quickly hides in the cupboard.)

(PENNY enters from the kitchen humming gaily. At the same moment CYRIL comes in from the hall carrying his overcoat and scarf.)

CYRIL *(suspiciously)* What are you up to?

PENNY Isn't he lovely! The Gregory Peck type. And not married either. *(She picks up the box of matches from the small table.)*

CYRIL It was pretty obvious the way you kept pumping him. If you'd left it to me I'd have found out all about Mrs. Benbow tactfully and without putting him on his guard.

PENNY *(crossing back to the kitchen)* He's the one I'm interested in . . not Mrs. Benbow. John Cunningham. The man from nowhere. The moment he rang the doorbell my heart went plinkety-plonk.

CYRIL I thought you said it was your stomach. *(He starts putting on his overcoat.)*

PENNY Where are you going?

CYRIL Back to the Beehive. I'm damned if I'm going to stay here and play gooseberry.

PENNY Cyril! *(She hugs him)* That's really sweet of you. You're my favourite brother. Don't hurry back will you.

CYRIL What time are Mother and Father coming in?

PENNY Oh I don't know. Not for some time yet, I hope.

CYRIL Make my apologies to Gregory Peck.

PENNY *(taking the scarf from his pocket and putting it round his neck)* Goodbye Cyril. Be as long as you like.

CYRIL How does he come to know so much about asteroids?

PENNY *(putting CYRIL'S hat on his head)* Off you go, Cyril. I'm wasting precious time.

CYRIL Do you think he's an astronomer or something?

PENNY *(opening the door and pushing him through)* Have a lovely time in the dear old Beehive. Lots and lots of long, long drinks.

CYRIL All right . . all right! There's no need to . . .

(Feebly protesting he is thrust out into the cold and foggy night.)

(PENNY, humming softly, turns out the main light, leaving the stage lit only by the soft shaded standard lamp and the warm glow from the fire. She shakes up the cushions on the U.S. armchair, takes two others from the D.S. armchair and puts them on the

floor in front of the fire. She crosses gaily to the kitchen and exits.)

PENNY *(as she closes the kitchen door behind her)* John, you've done it! You must be very strong!
(The cupboard opens and MISS CHAMBERS peers around the door. She is about to come out when she hears a sound on the landing. She hurriedly closes the door again.)

MRS. BENBOW *(appearing at the top of the stairs)* Blast that loose board. It always creaks.

MISS FAIRFAX *(descending the stairs close behind MRS. BENBOW)* Are you sure the coast is clear now?
(The kitchen door opens.)

MRS. BENBOW Look out.
(MRS. BENBOW and MISS FAIRFAX retreat hurriedly up the stairs again and exit.)
(Enter PENNY and JOHN D.L.)

PENNY We'll be much more comfortable in here.

JOHN *(observing the lighting arrangements)* So it seems. Where's your brother?

PENNY He had to go out. Suddenly. It was urgent. He was called away.

JOHN I see.

PENNY Let's sit by the fire. *(She takes his hand and draws him towards the fireplace.)*

JOHN What about the coffee?

PENNY We'll hear it when it whistles. Come on. *(She sits on the cushions on the floor.)*

JOHN All right. *(He sits in the upstage armchair)* Now *I'm* going to be inquisitive for a change. Tell me all about yourself.

PENNY There's not much to tell. I'm a shorthand typist. I work in the City. I live in the suburbs.

JOHN Oh no you don't. You live in the clouds.

PENNY Why do you say that?

JOHN Isn't it true?

PENNY *(after a slight pause)* Has someone been talking to you about me? Mrs. Benbow for instance?

JOHN *(with a laugh)* You're very attractive.

PENNY *(innocently)* Am I really? *(She moves even closer to the armchair.)*

JOHN As well you know. But a word of warning. Don't put all your cards on the table. Woman's art is to lie doggo and permit the male imagination to endow her with depths. You're not doing it you know.

PENNY *(not at all abashed)* Did you really mean it when you said you were thirty?

JOHN Of course.

PENNY *(considering him with her head on one side)* You don't look it.

25

JOHN *(laughing)* Thank you. I'm glad to hear that I carry my advanced years reasonably well.

PENNY Oh, I *like* you! You have a lovely laugh and such a nice sense of humour. It's funny but I feel as if I've known you for a long time.

JOHN My dear girl, we've only just met.

PENNY I know. Isn't it strange? *(She puts her hand on his.)*

JOHN Now look here, Junior Miss . . . *(He stops.)*

PENNY Yes . . . ?

JOHN I didn't come here to play postman's knock with a teenager.

PENNY *(softly)* I'm nearly twenty. *(There is a* SHRILL WHISTLE *from the kitchen.)*
Oh . . . Percolation ! ! !

JOHN *(rising)* Come along Miss Jones. *(He lifts her to her feet.)* Break for coffee.

PENNY Can't we just ignore it?

JOHN Not without ear plugs. *(He crosses to the kitchen.)* Come on before it explodes. *(He exits D.L.)*

PENNY *(with a wail as she follows him)* Just when we were getting to know each other! *(She exits D.L.)*
(The WHISTLING *stops.)* The GUY FAWKES *comes down the stairs. It goes to the cupboard and half opens the door but pauses with its hand on the knob, looking towards* CYRIL'S *bedroom D.R. It closes the cupboard door and exits D.R.)*
*(*MISS CHAMBERS *opens the cupboard door and is half out when she hears the loose board creak again on the landing. She quickly shuts herself in once more.)*

MRS. BENBOW *(appearing at the top of the stairs)* Now's our chance. Down the stairs and away.
*(*MISS FAIRFAX *is descending the stairs behind* MRS. BENBOW *when* JOHN *enters D.L. carrying the coffee percolator. He is minus his jacket and wearing a small frilly plastic apron.)*
(Mutual surprise.)
How long have you been here?

MISS FAIRFAX I thought you said you couldn't get along tonight?

JOHN I know, but where have you been all this time?

MRS. BENBOW We've been upstairs.

JOHN Upstairs!

MRS. BENBOW Yes. *(She switches on the main lights.)* If we'd known it was only you down here . . .

MISS FAIRFAX What happened to the recording?

JOHN Cancelled. The machine broke down so I came right over.

PENNY *(calling from the kitchen)* John . . . Oh, John . . .

MISS FAIRFAX Who's that?

JOHN That's Penny. The daughter. A nice kid . . very friendly.

MRS. BENBOW You haven't told her anything, have you?

JOHN I told her I wanted to discuss something with you but I didn't say what it was.

26

(PENNY enters D.L. with a tray containing two cups and saucers, milk jug and sugar bowl.)

PENNY *(her face falling)* Mrs. Benbow! You're back! *(She sees MISS FAIRFAX)* Oh . . . Good evening.

MRS. BENBOW Allow me to introduce you. My niece. Miss Jones.

MISS FAIRFAX Hello.

PENNY *(surprised)* Did you say your niece?

MRS. BENBOW My niece Miss Fairfax.

PENNY *(in an odd tone)* Oh.
(She puts the tray down on the large table. JOHN puts the percolator on the tray.)

MISS FAIRFAX However did you manage to domesticate John so quickly?

PENNY You know each other, do you?

MISS FAIRFAX We're old friends.

MRS. BENBOW They're both assisting me with a book I'm writing.

PENNY The one about . . .

MRS. BENBOW A study of tribal practices among primitive peoples. John's supplying me with material for my chapter on marriage customs and taboos in Wimbledon and Putney.

PENNY And where does Miss Fairfax come in?

MISS FAIRFAX They're using me for experiments.

PENNY Experiments!

JOHN Well, research really.

MISS FAIRFAX *(enjoying herself)* They're testing my reactions.

MRS. BENBOW Measuring her reflexes.

JOHN Finding out what makes the modern woman tick.

MISS FAIRFAX John's a past master at that.
(PENNY regards JOHN and MISS FAIRFAX thoughtfully.)

PENNY I see. Excuse me. I'll get some more cups and saucers. *(She exits D.L.)*

JOHN *(removing the apron)* Go easy with the leg pulling. She's very naive.

MISS FAIRFAX Girls of nineteen are not half as naive as you might think.

MRS. BENBOW *(to JOHN)* It's a pity you weren't here earlier. I wanted you to see over the house.

MISS FAIRFAX Never mind. *I've* got the general lay-out. Would you believe it, she even had a blueprint of the whole building upstairs in her bedroom.

MRS. BENBOW I want you both to study it carefully over the weekend. In the meantime memorise everything you see down here. The arrangement of the furniture, the pictures on the walls, everything.

JOHN You're a stickler for detail.

MRS. BENBOW It's attention to detail that makes all the difference in a thing like this.

(PENNY enters D.L. She carries a small tray containing two cups and saucers and a small plate of cakes. She has JOHN's jacket draped over her arm.)

JOHN   Here, let me take that. *(He takes the tray from her and sets it down on the table.)*

(PENNY hangs his jacket on the back of the chair left of the table.)

MISS FAIRFAX   This is very kind of you.

PENNY   That's all right. Will you pour them out John. I've brought some cakes as well in case you'd like something to eat. *(She offers the plate to MISS FAIRFAX.)*

MISS FAIRFAX   No thank you.

PENNY   Mrs. Benbow . . have a coconut eclair. Go on. I'm going to have one.

MRS. BENBOW   Not for me, thank you.

(PENNY takes one and starts to eat it.)

Ah, the careless confidence of the youthful appetite. Such faith in the gastric juices. Coconut eclairs taste much better at nineteen than at fifty.

JOHN   What were you doing at nineteen? Not eating coconut eclairs.

MRS. BENBOW   On my nineteenth birthday I ate wild honey, fried bees and locusts in the Sinai Desert. I was disguised as the younger son of an Armenian spice merchant and on my way to Mecca.

MISS FAIRFAX   My people always went to Broadstairs.

(The door U.C. opens.)

MRS. JONES   You mustn't mind. She's just naturally inquisitive.

(JOHN puts on his jacket, moving U.L. as he does so.)

MR. JONES   Inquisitive! She's a female ferret. *(He sees JOHN but shows no surprise.)* Tell me, young man, have *you* ever been asked how many women *your* grandfather kept?

JOHN   I can't say I have.

MRS. BENBOW   I must apologise for filling your home with uninvited guests. This is my niece—Miss Fairfax.

MISS FAIRFAX   I've heard a lot of nice things about you both from Mrs. Benbow . . .

(MRS. BENBOW gives her a look.)

. . . from Auntie.

MRS. JONES   How very kind.

MRS. BENBOW   And may I introduce Mr. John Cunningham.

JOHN   How do you do.

MR. JONES   You must come again some time. I'd like to hear more about this grandfather of yours. He sounds a bit of a lad. *(He moves to the fireplace, searching his pockets.)*

MRS. JONES   Isn't this fog terrible!

MISS FAIRFAX   Horrible. Cold and clammy.

PENNY   *(parting the curtains)* Goodness, it's so think! I can't even see the street lamps.

28

MRS. JONES *(removing her coat with* JOHN'S *assistance)* It's really dreadful. Fortunately we hadn't far to come but even so we twice took the wrong turning.

MR. JONES *(seeing* MISS FAIRFAX *for the first time)* How do you do. You haven't seen my cigar case anywhere have you?

MRS. BENBOW I've a new packet in a parcel from Yugoslavia I'll bring it down. *(She exits up the stairs.)*

(JOHN meanwhile is hanging up MRS. JONES'S *coat.)*

MRS. JONES *(above the table)* Do sit down, won't you? ·

MR. JONES What's that you're drinking? Coffee?

PENNY *(crossing above the table towards the kitchen)* I'll make a fresh pot.

MR. JONES The night's too chily and damp for coffee. *(He crosses to the sideboard.)* We need something warmer to keep the smog out. *(He takes a bottle of whisky from the sideboard cupboard and proceeds to fill several small glasses which are already set on top of the sideboard.)* Here's the very thing.

JOHN *(glancing at his watch)* I'm afraid I shall have to keep an eye on the time.

MR. JONES Must you? Why?

JOHN I shall soon have to think about making my way home to Chelsea.

PENNY Chelsea!

MR. JONES There's plenty of time yet. *(He hands a glass to* MRS. JONES.*)* I've had a dreary evening with a boring old busybody named Bumble-Cutts . . .

MRS. JONES Bunter-Cutts.

MR. JONES And it's a pleasant surprise to find such charming company here when I get back. *(He beams at* MISS FAIRFAX *and hands her a glass.)*

PENNY Do you live in Chelsea?

JOHN I do.

PENNY Not in a mews flat by the river?

JOHN As a matter of fact, I do.

PENNY Oh . . . !

JOHN How did you know?

PENNY I just did.

MR. JONES *(handing glass to* JOHN*)* We won't give Penny a glass. She's too young.

PENNY Oh, Father! I don't want any. I don't like the taste of it. But I do wish people would stop telling me I'm too young!

MR. JONES Here's health to you all . . . and damnation to Mrs. Gunter-Butts.

MISS FAIRFAX *(laughing)* I can't believe her name is really . . .

MRS. JONES It's Bunter-Cutts. Hyphenated.

JOHN Who is this Mrs. Bunter-Cutts?

MR. JONES She's a gorgon. A Medusa. And you should see her husband! A sad little man with an anxious look and a drooping

29

moustache. He creeps about in plimsols and never utters a word. But you feel him watching you out of the corners of his watery eyes while his wife asks you leading questions.

JOHN   And are there lots of little hyphenated Bunter-Cuttses?

MRS. JONES   They have a daughter. Arabella. She wasn't there tonight.

JOHN   Arabella Bunter-Cutts . . . It flows . . . it has a certain rhythm.

MRS. JONES   She's an odd girl.

MR. JONES   She couldn't be odder than her mother. Not unless she rides on a broomstick.

MRS. JONES   She's something of a problem child, I believe. Spends all her time reading detective thrillers and horror comics.

MISS FAIRFAX *(laughing)*   They sound quite a family.
(She glances at her watch.)
I don't really want to go but it is getting late. Will you share a taxi with me John?

JOHN   If we can get one.

MRS. JONES   You won't, I'm afraid. They all gave up hours ago. So did the buses.

JOHN   Then we'll have to go by tube.

PENNY   The station's right over the other side of the Common.

MR. JONES   By the time you've groped your way from here to there, the last train will have gone.

PENNY   How far do you have to go?

MISS FAIRFAX   Notting Hill Gate.

MR. JONES   You'll never get there. I wouldn't like to think of you trying.

MRS. JONES   You'd better stay the night. *(She turns to* PENNY*)* Miss Fairfax can have the room your Cousin Edith had when she was up for the Coronation.

MISS FAIRFAX   I wouldn't want to put you to so much trouble.

MRS. JONES   It won't be any trouble at all.
(She parts the curtains.)
We're certainly not going to turn you out into that. It's thicker than ever. I'd never forgive myself if you didn't stay.

PENNY   I can lend you a dressing gown if you like.

MISS FAIRFAX   Thank you Penny.

MR. JONES   That's one taken care of. Now we'll see what we can do about Mr. Carrington.

JOHN   Don't worry about me. If it comes to the worst I can walk.

PENNY   To Chelsea! John you couldn't. It's miles and miles. *(She turns to her mother)* What about that bed in the attic?

MRS. JONES   Yes, of course. It only needs making up.

MR. JONES   That's settled then. Give him a pair of my pyjamas.

MRS. JONES   I'll get some sheets. *(She turns towards the stairs.)*

JOHN   It's very good of you.   I'm afraid we're causing you a lot of inconvenience.

MRS. JONES *(with a smile)*   Of course you're not.

MISS FAIRFAX   I'll come and give you a hand.

(MRS. JONES and MISS FAIRFAX exit up the stairs.)

MR. JONES   Have another drink.   *(He refills JOHN's glass.)*

JOHN   Can't I make myself useful in some way?

PENNY *(eagerly)*   Oh yes.   You can help me in the attic.

MR. JONES   Where's Cyril?

PENNY   He went off to the Beehive and hasn't been seen since.

MR. JONES   I thought we were one short somewhere.

PENNY   Poor old Cyril.   He's having quite a night.   I expect he's feeling his way round the Odeon Car Park under the impression it's the High Street.

MR. JONES   I wonder if he'll have sense enough to count the gate-posts?   Knowing my son, I doubt it.   He's very unobservant, you know.   Takes after his mother.

(CYRIL enters U.C., choking. His hat, well down over his eyes, almost meets the edge of his scarf, which is wrapped round his face.)

Whoever's this?

CYRIL   Oh, my godfathers!   I thought I'd never see the old homestead again!

JOHN   Pretty thick, is it?

CYRIL   Thick!   It's like coming down a chimney!   You'd better stay the night.   You'll never get home in this.

JOHN   It's all arranged.   I'm shaking down up in the attic.

CYRIL   Good show.

PENNY   Come along John.

JOHN   Excuse me.

(PENNY and JOHN exit up the stairs.)

CYRIL *(unbuttoning his coat as he watches them go)*   Women are all the same.   Creatures of the jungle.   Why the attic anyway?   What's the matter with the spare room?

MR. JONES   We're putting Mrs. Benbow's niece in there.

CYRIL   Come again.   Mrs. Benbow's what?

MR. JONES   Her niece.

CYRIL *(hanging up his coat)*   She hasn't got one.

MR. JONES   Yes she has.   I've just seen her go upstairs.

CYRIL   That's odd.   What's she like?

MR. JONES   Charming.   Young . . . attractive.   Very much so.   She took quite a fancy to me.

CYRIL *(thoughtfully)*   Strange.

MR. JONES   What do you mean . . strange?

CYRIL   I wonder which way the wind blows.

MR. JONES   Under the street door.   Needs a strip of felt along the bottom.

CYRIL   Curiouser and curiouser.

31

MR. JONES What on earth are you talking about?

CYRIL Fishier and fishier.

(PENNY enters at the top of the stairs.)

MR. JONES *(plaintively)* Cyril, it's sometimes very difficult for me to get the gist of your conversation. *(He exits into the kitchen D.L.)*

PENNY What was that about?

CYRIL Mrs. Benbow's niece.

PENNY What about her?

CYRIL Didn't she say she had no living relatives?

PENNY Yes I know. That struck me too. Anyway she's nice. I like her. Throw me up a cushion.

CYRIL What for?

PENNY For John to rest his head on in the attic.

CYRIL Cushions on the floor, I see. *(He throws one up to her.)*

PENNY *(with sudden inspiration as she catches the cushion)* Cyril! Do you think she could be a spy!

CYRIL Who?

PENNY Mrs. Benbow! *(She comes quickly down the stairs.)* An agent for a foreign power! Why didn't we think of it before!

CYRIL Yes, it's possible. If only we knew what Father and Mrs. Benbow talked about down here in the middle of the night!

PENNY *(clutching CYRIL and looking nervously at the THING)* Cyril! Do you suppose the THING is really some sort of a . . .

(MR. JONES enters from the kitchen D.L.)

CYRIL *(sotto voice)* We'll talk about it in the morning.

(PENNY moves to the stairs. MRS. JONES enters at the top of the stairs with MRS. BENBOW who is wearing pyjamas and dressing gown.)

MRS. BENBOW That's most accommodating of you. *(To MR. JONES)* I hear you're putting them up for the night.

MR. JONES We could do no less.

CYRIL I'm looking forward to meeting your niece, Mrs. Benbow.

MRS. JONES You'll have to wait until the morning, Cyril. She's gone to bed.

MRS. BENBOW I'm off too. *(She hands a packet over the balustrade to MR. JONES)* Here are some cigars for you. The Serbs call these Yerbashas. The peasant women smoke them to alleviate the pangs of child-birth.

MR. JONES Thank you. *(Taking the packet)* I'll give them a trial.

MRS. BENBOW Good-night all.

(There is a chorus of "Goodnight" during which MRS. BENBOW and PENNY exit and MRS. JONES comes down the stairs.)

MRS. JONES Now what about you Cyril? *(Collecting glasses)* Shall I get you a hot drink and something to eat?

CYRIL No thanks' Mother. I'm turning in.

MRS. JONES Sleep well.

CYRIL *(yawning)* Thank Heaven it's Sunday tomorrow. *(He exits into his bedroom D.R.)*

MRS. JONES You won't forget the front door, will you?

MR. JONES I'll do it now.

(He moves to the main door and bolts it. Meanwhile MRS. JONES collects the last of the glasses from the top of the THING. She stands for a moment, tray in hand, regarding the THING. MR. JONES comes back from the hall.)

MRS. JONES I do think my husband's clever.

MR. JONES I'm glad you're beginning to realise it.

MRS. JONES I've always known it.

MR. JONES Where should I be without your subtle flattery? *(He kisses her on the forehead.)*

MRS. JONES *(pleased)* Careful now. You'll make me drop the tray.

MR. JONES Let me take it. *(He takes the tray from her and moves towards the kitchen door.)*

MRS. JONES Is Lucifer in or out? *(She switches off the standard lamp.)*

MR. JONES *(as he exits, leaving the kitchen door ajar)* Lucy . . . Lucy . . . Lucy . . . Oh, there you are. *(He returns, closing the door.)* He's asleep in his box under the clothes rail.

MRS. JONES Are you sure that clothes rail is safe? *(She switches off the hall light.)*

MR. JONES Of course it's safe. I mended it, didn't I?

MRS. JONES You don't think all those towels are too heavy for it?

MR. JONES *(switching off the main lights)* Not now I've fixed new pulleys in the ceiling. *(He puts an arm round her shoulders as they go upstairs.)*

MRS. JONES I'd hate it to come down with a crash.

MR. JONES Don't worry. It's perfectly safe.

(They exit. The stage is lit only by the red glow from the fire and a thin shaft of light from the landing.)

(Offstage, the Grandfather Clock intones TWELVE MIDNIGHT— though whether this is really the hour is open to question. As the last stroke dies away the CUPBOARD starts to creak open.)

(From the KITCHEN comes a LOUD CRASH and an ear-splitting FELINE YOWL as the clothes rail descends upon LUCIFER. The CUPBOARD closes quickly. The noise causes CYRIL to open his bedroom door. He has removed his jacket and now wears a flamboyant dressing gown. He crosses to the kitchen and exits.)

(Immediately the Kitchen Door closes behind CYRIL, the GUY FAWKES enters from CYRIL's bedroom.)

(There is a single chime from the Grandfather Clock offstage as GUY FAWKES crosses the stage and exits up the stairs.)

(The moment GUY FAWKES has disappeared MISS CHAMBERS emerges from the CUPBOARD, ascends the stairs, sees GUY FAWKES returning and conceals herself hurriedly behind the heavy red velvet

curtain which hangs at the angle of the staircase. GUY FAWKES
enters down the stairs, goes to the CUPBOARD *and brings out the
chair.)*

(The offstage Grandfather Clock chimes twice. GUY FAWKES
*sets the chair centre stage, then cautiously ascends the stairs again
and exits.)*

*(*MISS CHAMBERS *peers out from behind the curtain but withdraws
her head abruptly as the Kitchen Door opens.* CYRIL *enters from
the Kitchen and crosses the stage, looking back over his shoulder
towards the stairs. He walks into the chair.)*

CYRIL Blast ! ! ! *(He hops about on one foot, making anguished
faces and rubbing his shin.)*

*(*MR. JONES *gives a hollow strangled cough off U.L.* CYRIL *limps
to the foot of the stairs and listens.* MR. JONES *coughs again and*
MRS. BENBOW'S *voice is heard off U.L.* CYRIL *looks around for
a hiding place suitable for eavesdropping and hurriedly enters the*
CUPBOARD *closing the door.)*

*(*GUY FAWKES *hurries down the stairs and sits in the wheelchair.*
MRS. BENBOW *and* MR. JONES *enter cautiously at the top of the
stairs.* MRS. BENBOW *enters first. She turns at the foot of the
stairs and shushes* MR. JONES *who is coughing wheezily.)*

MR. JONES It's this smog. It gets in everywhere. *(He has
removed his jacket.)*

MRS. BENBOW Ssh! You're making too much noise! *(She backs
into the chair.)* BLAST the . . . Fifth of November ! ! !

MR. JONES Ssh! Not so loud!

MRS. BENBOW I shall be glad when this thing has gone up in
flames. I've already put it away twice this evening.

MR. JONES Someone must have brought it out again. Cyril, I
expect.

MRS. BENBOW *(following her own train of thought)* There are dark
places in the mind of primitive man.

MR. JONES Oh, he's all right. A bit forgetful but a nice enough
lad when you get to know him.

MRS. BENBOW I've witnessed strange ceremonies in the mud kraals
of the Congo. These effigies give me an uneasy feeling somewhere
between the pit of my stomach and my soul.

MR. JONES Do they? Wheel it back in the cupboard and I'll
lock the door. *(He opens the cupboard door. It can stay in
here until we take it out and burn it on our bonfire.)*

*(*MRS. BENBOW *wheels* GUY FAWKES *into the cupboard, where*
CYRIL *is already concealed behind coats hanging at the back.)*

I've made one of these every November since Cyril was a boy of five.
I remember one year he wanted to take the Guy to bed with him
instead of his teddy bear. Yes, he actually wanted to spend the
night with it. *(He cloks the door and hangs the key on a hook.)*

MRS. BENBOW That's highly significant. It indicates an instinctive
transposition of a sublimated father fixation, linked with a

34

subconscious desire for image worship. Possibly pre-natal in origin.

MR. JONES That wouldn't surprise me at all.

MRS. BENBOW *(regarding the* THING*)* I rang up Zelnicker today. He was most impressed.

MR. JONES Good.

MRS. BENBOW Shokolovsky thinks this will cause nothing less than a revolution.

MR. JONES I'm delighted to hear it.

MRS. BENBOW I'm meeting them both tomorrow to settle the final details. Will you come?

MR. JONES. No, no. I leave that side of it entirely to you. *(Picking up the whisky bottle.)* How about a nightcap? Bring a couple of glasses and we'll have it in the kitchen. We don't want anyone to hear us.

MRS. BENBOW *(taking two glasses from the sideboard)* Quite right. Discretion must be our watchword. Especially at this stage.
(They exit into the kitchen D.L The Door Handle of the locked cupboard rattles unhappily two or three times. PENNY *enters at the top of the stairs. She is wearing pyjamas and dressing-gown.)*

PENNY But I did. I'm sure I did.
*(*JOHN *enters. He is wearing a pair of* MR. JONES'S *pyjamas underneath his jacket.)*

JOHN What sort of a noise?

PENNY A crash. And a thump. And then somebody screamed.

JOHN It sounds like chapter one of a nightmare.

PENNY It could be burglars.

JOHN It could be Miss Jones' fervid imagination.

PENNY You don't believe I heard a noise at all, do you!

JOHN I didn't say that.

PENNY No, but you think it! You think I thought it would be a good way to get you down here after everyone else had gone to bed.

JOHN Let's not go into what you think I thought you thought. There's no telling where that might lead us.

PENNY Oh . . . you're horrible.

JOHN *(chuckling)* I know.

PENNY I don't care whether you believe me or not. I did hear a noise.

JOHN Look, Miss Jones. I'm just as susceptible as the next man. If you want me to hold your hand in the dark, I will. But let's be quite clear on one point.

PENNY What do you mean?

JOHN Like most men I run a mile from forward females. I prefer to pursue rather than be the quarry.

PENNY You have me taped, haven't you? With a label round my neck saying . . " Teenager . . . emotionally overdeveloped . . . amorous."

35

JOHN *(indicating the empty room by way of reply)* What do you want me to do with all these burglars?

PENNY You can scoff if you like but there's something very peculiar going on in this house. What's more, Father and your Mrs. Benbow are mixed up in it.

JOHN What makes you say that?

PENNY All sorts of things. First there was Foxy-Face.

(Offstage Grandfather Clock chimes once.)

JOHN Who?

PENNY Well, I call her that. Cyril and I spotted her a few days ago, hiding behind a tree on the other side of the road, just as it was getting dark. She had her collar turned up to hide her face and I'm sure she was watching the house.

JOHN How very odd!

PENNY When she saw us at the window she turned and hurried away. I thought at first it might have been one of Cyril's girl friends but he said No, she wasn't his type.

(Offstage Grandfather Clock chimes twice.)

Frankly John, I'm worried. Father's not very practical and I'm afraid he may have got himself mixed up with some shady characters.

(JOHN laughs.)

You can laugh but I don't think Mrs. Benbow is what she pretends to be.

JOHN Oh?

PENNY You know all about her. I'm sure you do. What is she up to? Why is she staying here?

JOHN I can't tell you that . . . not at the moment.

PENNY Not at the moment . . . ? Then you *do* know what it's all about!

JOHN *(evasively)* Well . . .

PENNY Why is she so interested in Father's invention?

JOHN *(turning towards the stairs)* I really think it's time we went back to our beds.

(PENNY takes hold of the lapels of his jacket to stop him. He holds her by the shoulders.)

PENNY You know what's going on and yet you won't tell me. Don't you trust me?

(There is a pause. JOHN tightens his arms around her.)

JOHN *(softly)* Penny . . . *(For a moment it seems that he is about to kiss her. He releases her and draws away.)* There's nothing for you to worry about.

PENNY You *don't* trust me. You think I'm just a child.

JOHN *(stopping and turning two steps up the stairs)* I think you're a very disturbing person.

PENNY Do you John?

JOHN It's getting late. *(He goes up two more steps.)*

PENNY Please don't go. *(There is a pause as she comes slowly up*

36

the first two steps.) Something strange happened when you rang our doorbell.

JOHN   What was it?

PENNY   I felt all quivery and goosefleshy.

JOHN   There's a lot of flu about.

(PENNY looks woebegone.)

Are you feeling all right?

PENNY *(in a small voice)*   No.

JOHN   I think you've caught a chill.   *(He comes down to her and puts an arm around her shoulders.)*   Why, you're shivering.   You ought to be tucked up in bed.

PENNY   Oh, you're so good to me!   *(She heaves a deep sigh of contentment, closes her eyes and leans her head against his chest. JOHN is struck by a sudden suspicion.)*

JOHN   Did you *really* hear a noise?

(PENNY lifts her head, a sphinc-like expression on her face.)

PENNY   I'm glad there's no whistling coffee-pot this time.   *(Her arms go about his neck.   They are about to kiss when . . . . A SNEEZE is heard from inside the cupboard.)*

JOHN   What was that?

(The SNEEZE is repeated, this time very loudly.)

CYRIL *(within the cupboard)*   Oh my Godfathers ! ! !

(Pandemonium within the cupboard. Clattering, banging, tins falling, etc.   CYRIL is heard voicing distress and alarm.)

PENNY   That's Cyril's voice!   *(She crosses to the cupboard.)*

JOHN   What's he doing in there?

PENNY *(finding the door locked)*   He's locked in!

CYRIL *(in terror)*   UGH!   IT'S ALIVE!   LET ME OUT!

(JOHN quickly takes the key from the hook and turns it in the lock.   CYRIL and GUY FAWKES endeavour to burst out of the cupboard simultaneously and there is a scrum in the doorway as they become entangled with JOHN and PENNY.)

UGH!   KEEP IT OFF!   IT'S COME TO LIFE!

(PENNY screams.   MRS. BENBOW and MR. JONES enter from the kitchen.)

MRS. BENBOW   Who's making all this noise?

(Offstage Grandfather Clock starts to chime sonorously and rapidly, continuing to do so throughout the following business.)

(JOHN switches on the main lights.   The GUY FAWKES rushes to the door U.C., pulls the bolt and starts to open the door.   JOHN grabs the GUY FAWKES and slams the door shut again.   The GUY FAWKES wrenches itself free from JOHN and makes for the stairs, pushing CYRIL aside as it does so.   Meanwhile excited ad lib is heard from all.)

(CYRIL catches at the GUY FAWKES' sleeve.   The GUY FAWKES pulls away but the delay has enabled JOHN to catch up with it halfway up the stairs.   JOHN overpowers it, aided by CYRIL, and

37

brings it to Centre Stage, right of the table. The Grandfather Clock stops chiming.)

JOHN Let's take a look at him. *(He removes the* GUY FAWKES *black slouch hat.)* Come on. The game's up.

CYRIL *(nervously)* Yes, you'd better come quietly.

JOHN Now we'll have this off. *(He removes the mask from the* GUY FAWKES' *face.)* Good Heavens!

CYRIL What's the matter?

JOHN It's a woman!

PENNY It's her!

CYRIL Her? Who's her?

PENNY *(pointing excitedly)* It's HER! It's Foxy-Face!

CYRIL Good Lord! So it is!

*(*MISS FAIRFAX *enters at the top of the stairs in pyjamas and dressing gown.)*

MISS FAIRFAX What's been happening here?

CYRIL *(turning at the sound of her voice)* Elisabeth! *(He gapes in amazement.)*

MISS FAIRFAX *(in great surprise)* Cyril ! ! Darling ! ! What are *you* doing here?

*(*MISS CHAMBERS' *black-gloved hand emerges from behind the staircase curtains unnoticed and gropes for the main switch by the fuse box.)*

CYRIL What am *I* . . . ? *(With an audible click the lights go off and chaos ensues. There is indiscriminate seething and struggling as the Offstage Grandfather Clock starts to chime midnight again very rapidly indeed. Above the confused shouts* JOHN'S *voice is heard.)*

JOHN Look out! The window!

(There is a crash of glass as GUY FAWKES *exits through the window U.R.)*

QUICK CURTAIN

ACT THREE

(The following evening. CYRIL *is sitting despondently at the large table.* PENNY *is in the hall, removing her coat, gloves, etc., having only just come in.*

PENNY   There could be half a dozen explanations.

CYRIL   That's what I keep telling myself. I can't think of *one*.

PENNY   There was no need for you to go stalking off to bed last night in high dudgeon.

CYRIL   High dudgeon! Me? High dudgeon!

PENNY   Yes, you. Very high old dudgeon indeed.

CYRIL   That wasn't dudgeon. That was confusion. You must admit it is a bit bewildering when you find the girl you love secretly staying the night under your own roof, posing in pyjamas as a non-existent and mythological niece . . . and all she does is laugh like a drain and say she can't explain just yet!

PENNY   Oh well, if you will go taking umbrage every time you find a woman telling little white lies in pyjamas . . .

CYRIL   It wasn't a little white one. It was a whopping great big one.

PENNY   I had a long talk with her over breakfast while you were snoring like a man sawing logs. She said it was all very simple really.

CYRIL   I daresay it is. If you ask me it wasn't just coincidence that she and this John Cunningham happened to be staying here on the same night.

PENNY   What do you mean?

CYRIL   It's obvious, isn't it?

PENNY   Don't talk nonsense. John couldn't possibly be . . . *(She stops suddenly)* At least, I don't think . . . Oh, Lord. She said they were old friends. But I don't believe it. You must be off your rocker.

CYRIL   It wouldn't be surprising if I was. Nobody seems to realise what a terrible time I had cooped up in that cupboard. I'll never forget the awful moment when it suddenly sneezed . . . right there beside me in the dark. My blood ran cold and I nearly jumped out of my skin! Do you know there are white streaks in my hair this morning!

PENNY   Serves you right. What a silly place to put yourself.

CYRIL   I wanted to be near enough to hear what Mrs. Benbow was up to with the THING. It was your idea in the first place.

PENNY   My idea? What was?

CYRIL   You told me how you stood and watched them from the landing.

PENNY   Standing on the landing's one thing. Lurking in the ...cupboard's another. Anyway, she's coming back this evening to see you.

39

CYRIL *(jumping up)* She is! When?

PENNY She said round about seven.

CYRIL It's seven now!

(Offstage Grandfather Clock chimes once.)

Oh be quiet! Why didn't you tell me!

PENNY This is the first chance I've had. *I* wasn't in this morning and you were out this afternoon.

CYRIL I've been trying to ring her all day!

(Doorbell.)

PENNY I expect that's her now. I'll leave you to it. *(She moves to the stairs.)* You'll probably find there's a perfectly straightforward explanation of the whole thing. *(She exits up the stairs.)*

CYRIL *(moving to the door)* That's what I'm afraid of! *(He opens the door.)*

MISS FAIRFAX *(coming straight in)* Cyril! Darling! *(She takes him by the hand and leads him into the room.)*

CYRIL *(meanwhile)* I'm glad you've come back. There are things I must know. Why . . .

(She kisses him . . . long and lingering.)

MISS FAIRFAX Oh, Cyril, you're wonderful!

CYRIL Am I darling?

MISS FAIRFAX Do you remember the first time you kissed me under the mulberry tree?

CYRIL I should say I do. The rain kept dripping down my neck . . . I was standing in a puddle and my feet were like ice.

MISS FAIRFAX It's such a comfort to know that you trust me.

CYRIL *(doubtfully)* Do I darling? Well now, wait a minute. About last night . . .

MISS FAIRFAX Darling, I owe you an explanation.

CYRIL You certainly do. Why were you masquerading as Mrs. Benbow's niece?

MISS FAIRFAX That was her idea, not mine.

CYRIL Her idea! Has she got some sort of hold over you?

MISS FAIRFAX Of course not. It was just that she didn't want anyone to know what John and I *really* came here for.

(CYRIL splutters incoherently.)

Oh Cyril, I was so looking forward to our evening together. There I was waiting in the Beehive, all warm and expectant. Then Mrs. Benbow came in to tell me John couldn't get away and I must come instead.

CYRIL Where?

MISS FAIRFAX Here. That's when I found out the Joneses were real people.

CYRIL Of course we're real people! I'm not made of marzipan.

MISS FAIRFAX But I had no idea you were one of the family.

CYRIL The more you explain the less I understand.

...*(PENNY enters at the top of the stairs with a copy of the "Radio Times.")*

40

PENNY *(at the top of the stairs)* Look! Look what I've just found. It was lining the bottom of my wardrobe!

CYRIL What is it?

PENNY *(descending the stairs)* Hullo Elisabeth. Did you know about this?

CYRIL *(mystified)* " The Radio Times " . . . . ?

PENNY It's an old copy. Last March. *(She points)* Just there.

CYRIL *(reading)* " The Dark Planet." A radio serial in twelve parts. Episode Six. The Space Fleet Lands on Mars . . . . Yes, I remember hearing this. It was jolly good. What about it?

(PENNY points in silence. CYRIL reads and then whistles.)
No wonder he . . . .

PENNY *(to ELISABETH)* *Did* you know?

MISS FAIRFAX Well . . . .

(Doorbell. CYRIL opens the door.)

JOHN Good evening Cyril. Is Penny at home?

CYRIL Ah! The man himself!

PENNY Come right in.

(JOHN enters. CYRIL closes the door.)
Tell us more about asteroids.

CYRIL How are things on the dark side of the moon?

JOHN *(coming into the room)* On the . . . !

PENNY Seen any green-faced Martians lately?

CYRIL How did they get out of that volcano on Venus? I missed the next episode.

JOHN I do believe I'm rumbled.

MISS FAIRFAX *(laughing)* The cat's out of the bag . . . at least as far as you're concerned.

JOHN Did you . . . ?

MISS FAIRFAX Not guilty.

JOHN Then how . . . ?

PENNY *(holding out the "Radio Times")* " The Dark Planet." A radio serial in twelve parts . . produced by John Cunningham.

JOHN So you've unearthed my guilty secret.

PENNY I don't know about that. Shall we say we've stumbled upon one of them. You do know more than you'll admit, don't you?

JOHN That's very much a leading question.

PENNY Suppose you start at the beginning.

(MISS FAIRFAX and JOHN exchange a look.)

CYRIL Come on. Both of you. Divulge.

JOHN Do you think we should?

MISS FAIRFAX We *should* . . . but I'm not so sure that we can. Not until Mrs. Benbow gives the word.

CYRIL Mrs. Benbow again! Why does everything refer back to Mrs. Benbow?

PENNY And why is she so interested in the THING?

JOHN   In what?

PENNY   The THING.

JOHN   What thing?

CYRIL   This. *(He indicates the* THING *and removes the sheet.)*

JOHN   What is it?

PENNY   We don't know.

CYRIL   He won't tell us.

JOHN   Who?

PENNY   Father. Don't pretend you're in the dark too.

JOHN *(to* MISS FAIRFAX*)* Do *you* know what it is?

MISS FAIRFAX   I haven't a clue.

CYRIL   Doesn't anybody know!

JOHN   Cross my heart . . . *I'm* baffled.

PENNY   But last night you admitted you knew!

JOHN   Knew what?

PENNY   More than you said.

JOHN   Who did?

PENNY   *You* did!

JOHN   *I* did?

CYRIL   I shall go mad . . I shall go mad! *(He sits at the large table.)*

JOHN   We seem to be at cross purposes.

MISS FAIRFAX   John, we shall *have* to tell them.

JOHN   I think you're right.

PENNY   Then you do know what Mrs. Benbow's up to with the THING?

JOHN AND MISS FAIRFAX *(together)* No. We don't.

CYRIL   I shall go quietly stark raving gibbering. Suppose we all speak very slowly and give each other time to think. *Who* is talking about *what?*

JOHN   Well you've heard of Mrs. Dale's Diary?

CYRIL   I give up. I give up. *(He buries his head in his hands.)*

PENNY   Of course.

JOHN   Five years it's been running now with ten million pairs of ears glued to it every afternoon. And on Television there's the Grove Family.

CYRIL   Everyone to his taste. What about it?

JOHN   I have been engaged to produce a commercial television series which the sponsors hope will run as long as the Dales and the Groves put together.

PENNY   Congratulations but what has that to do with us?

JOHN   The programme will be called . . ." Mrs. Jones' Journal." The leading characters will be Father, Mother, Cyril the son and Penny the daughter.

CYRIL AND PENNY   What ! ! !

MISS FAIRFAX   Not forgetting Lucifer the cat.

PENNY   You mean you want us to appear on TV?

JOHN   No, we have actors already chosen to impersonate you but the inspiration and origin of the whole thing will be here in this house.

CYRIL   Why pick on us?

JOHN   Quite by chance. Mrs. Benbow happened to meet your father just after she'd been asked to write the script.

PENNY   Has Mrs. Benbow been writing about *us?*

CYRIL   Do you mean to say that for the last three months we've been raw material for Commercial TV?

PENNY   I'm not sure I altogether like the idea.

JOHN   She always takes her characters from life. I expect you've read some of her books. Most women have.

PENNY   I didn't know she'd written any yet.

JOHN   Not under her real name.

MISS FAIRFAX   The're very popular and very good of their type type too. " Love in a Warm Climate " . . . " I Capture the Citadel " . . . " Three Coins in a Lily Pond " . . .

JOHN   " The Garden of Ali " . . .

PENNY *(open-mouthed with amazement)*   " The Garden of . . ! "

JOHN   " Love among the Scented Blossoms " . . .

PENNY   " Love among the . . . ! "

MISS FAIRFAX   Then there are the Millicent books. " Millicent the Girl " . . .

PENNY *(faintly)*   " Millicent the Wife " . . .

MISS FAIRFAX   " Millicent the Mother " . . .

PENNY *(in awe-stricken tones)*   Jonathan Gabriel! In this very house . . . under this very roof!

CYRIL *(rising)*   Don't take any notice of me. I'm just passing through . . . *(He crosses to the sideboard and picks up Penny's library book.)*   Does this mean that Mrs. Benbow is really the fellow who makes thousands a year simply by . . . *(He opens the fly leaf)* . . . " impaling the heart of woman on the sharp thorns of his . . . *(He turns to the back inside cover)* . . . passionate insight." ?

JOHN   That's the man. Or rather, the woman.

CYRIL *(throwing the book away)*   And me working in a bank!

PENNY   But that makes all the difference! If Mrs. Benbow . . . I mean Jonathan Gabriel . . . Oh, she's a wonderful writer!

JOHN   Living here incognito has enabled her to assimilate the authentic family atmosphere which we hope will make " Mrs. Jones' Journal " a great success.

PENNY   How far has she got with it?

JOHN   She's written twelve episodes so far and the first one goes into rehearsal next week.

CYRIL   The private life of Cyril Jones exposed to the multitudes!

JOHN   We're building a permanent set in the studio as an exact replica of this house, with identical furniture, carpets and fittings. We're even matching the wallpaper on the landing and the pattern on the bathmat.

PENNY   Well blow me down! *(She sits at the table.)*

JOHN   Mrs. Benbow wanted me to come here yesterday and take a look around.   At first I thought I couldn't make it so I suggested she get hold of my secretary instead.   I knew Elisabeth was meeting someone at the Beehive but I had no idea it was Cyril.

CYRIL   Your secretary!

MISS FAIRFAX   I type Mrs. Benbow's manuscripts and try to decipher the heiroglyphic scrawl she calls handwriting.

CYRIL   *(taking her hand and leading her towards his room D.R.)* Come and look at my stamp album.   Now you're unmasked there are things I have to discuss with you . . . alone and right now.   *(He stops and turns to* JOHN*)*   By the way . . do we get anything out of this?

JOHN   The sponsors are a wealthy Tinned Food firm.   They'll pay a useful fee to the Joneses for the use of their name and background.   It's all arranged.

MISS FAIRFAX   Darling Cyril, I knew you were a man of the world.

CYRIL   *(as they exit)*   There are very few flies on the Joneses.

*(*MISS FAIRFAX *and* CYRIL *exit D.R.   There is a pause.)*

JOHN   It's very quiet suddenly, isn't it?   *(*PENNY *makes no reply.)* How are you, Penny?

PENNY   Oh . . . I'm fine.

JOHN   I really must apologise for rushing off this morning without saying good-bye.

PENNY   That's all right.   I didn't come down till after ten.   Cyril died until twelve.   I'm glad you came back.   I ought to apologise too.

JOHN   For what?

PENNY   Making such a pass at you.   I expect you found it very tiresome.

JOHN   *(amused)*   I wouldn't say that.

PENNY   I must have seemed very ingenious . . . or do I mean ingenuous?

JOHN   You were both.   But you were also very sweet and I was flattered by your attentions.

PENNY   Oh, you say such *nice* things!   You'd make a wonderful husband.   Why hasn't somebody landed you?

JOHN   Hooks have been baited.   But I've never yet found the right woman.

PENNY   Perhaps you're too choosy.

JOHN   I wonder.

PENNY   I expect you only fall for still waters women.

JOHN   What are they?

PENNY   Enigmatic slinky types who run very deep.   That's the impressionable schoolboy in you.   It's high time you grew up.

JOHN   You may be right.

PENNY   I wish I knew how to be seductive and beckoning.   Like . . . whoever it was . . . sitting on her rock . . luring sailors to their doom.

44

JOHN *(laughing)* I can't quite see you doing that. There's something far too candid and honest about you.
PENNY *(unenthusiastically)* Candour ... honesty. Those are things a man only looks for in his sister.
JOHN *(quietly)* Not necessarily. Besides, you have other qualities as well. A warm generosity of spirit ... a very natural and unforced charm ... and a great deal of purely physical attractions.
PENNY Do you really mean that?
JOHN In five years time you'll be quite a woman.
PENNY *(glumly)* Five years. *(She rises and moves to the left end of the table, turned a little away from him so that he cannot see her face.)* You said last night I was disturbing. Do you remember?
JOHN I remember.
PENNY I don't feel disturbing. Not any more. I'm too disturbed.
JOHN Are you. Why?
PENNY *(in a small sad voice, not far from tears, as she turns to face him)* I think it's because I've fallen in love with you ... No, don't say anything. I know you don't believe me. Like everybody else you think I'm too young to know when I'm in love.
JOHN How can you know? We've only just met.
PENNY I fell in love with you last night, the moment you rang the doorbell. As I went to the door to open it I knew who'd be standing there.
JOHN But ... but you'd never even seen me before!
PENNY No, I hadn't. But I'd been waiting for you for a long time. All my life I think.
JOHN All your life ... you're not twenty yet!
PENNY I shall be next year. April the sixteenth.
JOHN *(after a slight pause)* Are you really sincere about this?
PENNY Yes.
JOHN Good Lord, I believe you are.
PENNY I'm not really a flighty wench. I don't go around flinging myself at men. It's just that music plays inside me whenever I think of you. November seems like June and the grass in the garden is greener than I've ever known it before.
JOHN *(gently)* Am I the cause of all that?
PENNY And more besides ... It wasn't flu that made me shiver .... Darling, will you marry me?
JOHN *(backing away in alarm)* Just a moment! I'm what is known as a confirmed bachelor. I'm a slippers and pipe man ... I go for walks with a wire-haired fox terrier ...
PENNY *(following him as he backs away)* Woof! Woof!
JOHN *(still retreating)* But I'm much older than you are ...
PENNY You're bigger too.
JOHN My love life is complicated enough as it is! I'm already as good as engaged to half a dozen women ...
PENNY Wild oats. You can keep them as a hobby.
JOHN Penny ... *(Embarrassed yet touched he searches for the*

45

right words) . . . Penny, listen to me. I know you've heard and read a lot about love at first sight. But it doesn't really happen. *(She is about to speak but he puts his hand gently over her lips.)* You may *think* it does . . . but it doesn't . . . not really.

PENNY Not to you it doesn't. But it has to me.

JOHN *(softly)* You've such a lot to learn, Penny.

PENNY *(closing her eyes. She is very close to him)* Yes . . . teacher. *(They are about to kiss when they are interrupted by a rapid series of very loud explosions from the kitchen and are once again jarred rudely from romance to reality.)*

*(*MR. JONES *enters hurriedly from the kitchen, clasping in his arms a cardboard box and half a dozen empty bottles with stick rockets protruding from them. He looks nervously over his shoulder towards the now silent kitchen.)*

PENNY What's happening in there?

MR. JONES It's . . .

(There is a final and tremendous explosion which makes all three start and all but causes MR. JONES *to drop the bottles.)*

It's called a jumping devil-cracker. I must have put it down on the hot plate.

*(*CYRIL *and* MISS FAIRFAX *enter in alarm D.R.)*

CYRIL What's going on?

MR. JONES Let's send up a few rockets while we're waiting.

PENNY Waiting for what?

MR. JONES Did I say waiting?

PENNY You did.

MR. JONES Well . . waiting for your mother to come back.

CYRIL Where is mother? I haven't seen her all day.

MR. JONES *(evasively)* Oh she's . . . out. Give me a hand with these will you?

*(*JOHN *takes the box and the bottles from him and puts them on the large table.)*

PENNY Father, I sometimes wonder if you're really quite as vague as you seem.

MR. JONES Whatever do you mean?

PENNY Strange things have happened. Foxy-face, the two foreigners, midnight visits to the woodshed . . .

CYRIL Who's Sokolovsky?

PENNY *(indicating the* THING*)* Why sealing wax on the knots?

CYRIL Who's Tzelnicker?

PENNY The time has come. *(She points an accusing finger at the* THING.*)* What IS it?

MR. JONES Let's go and light the bonfire. *(He moves towards the window.)*

PENNY Cyril . . . get the bread knife. We'll saw through the ropes.

MR. JONES Oh no! You mustn't do that!

CYRIL Why not?

MR. JONES It's meant to be a surprise.

CYRIL It could hardly be anything else.

MR. JONES *(producing a firework from the box and handing it to
JOHN)* Would you like to try one of these fiery cascades?

PENNY Cyril . . . the bread knife.

CYRIL Right. *(He makes purposefully for the kitchen.)*

MR. JONES No, wait! *(There is a pause.)* If you really insist
. . . . I'll tell you. *(He clears his throat)* As a matter of fact
it's a . . . .
(MRS. JONES burst in U.C. She is very excited and happy.)

MRS. JONES Reg! I'm so pleased for you! I can hardly believe
it's true!

PENNY What is it?

CYRIL What's happened?

MR. JONES Was everything all right?

MRS. JONES They couldn't have been nicer.

PENNY Who couldn't?

MRS. JONES *(delving into her handbag)* I've got it!

CYRIL For Pete's sake Mother! *What* have you got?

MRS. JONES *(producing a cheque and brandishing it triumphantly)*
I've got it! Isn't it wonderful! *(She hugs MR. JONES gleefully.
He takes the cheque and stares at it. He too is highly delighted.)*

PENNY *(tapping her mother's shoulder)* Remember us?

CYRIL We live here. Your kith and kin . . . remember?

MRS. JONES *(sitting)* Wait until I get my breath back. They've
bought Father's invention.

PENNY AND CYRIL What! The THING!

MRS. JONES Oh, it's been such a day! You tell them what it is.

MR. JONES *(with transparent modesty)* It was just a little idea I
had. It's a device for separating smooth peas from wrinkled
peas.

PENNY For doing what!

MR. JONES Yes, you see some peas come out of their pods spherical
and others are crinkly and corrugated.

CYRIL *(wiggling his finger in his ear)* I don't think I can hear very
well.

MRS. JONES *(proudly)* It's been bought by the biggest pea-proces-
sing company in England.

MR. JONES You feed the peas in through the funnel at the back,
they travel down a spiral shaft on to a centrifugally controlled
moving belt rotating and vibrating in such a way that the round
peas roll off and come out through an opening here on the right.
The others are carried along to the ejector and come out through
a corresponding aperture here on the left.

PENNY Let me see that cheque. *(She takes it and reads what is
written on it.)* Ye Gods!

CYRIL How much?

MRS. JONES Five thousand pounds for the patent. Isn't it exciting!

PENNY Crikey Moses! *(She regards the* THING *with awe and reverence.)*

CYRIL Five thousand pounds! *(He shakes his father warmly by the hand.)* Congratulations Father. I always said you were a genius.

MISS FAIRFAX How wonderful for you Mr. Jones.

JOHN *(to* MRS. JONES*)* You must be very proud of him.

MR. JONES Maud and Mrs. Benbow were the brains and the business side of the whole thing. I simply invented it . . . but they sold it.

CYRIL I suggest we celebrate. It isn't every night that Father hits the jackpot.

PENNY *(hugging her Father)* I had no idea I had such a clever parent. Is that why those men came to see you?

MR. JONES I gave them a demonstration. They were most impressed.

JOHN *(to* CYRIL*)* Do you feel strong enough to carry one end of a crate of beer?

CYRIL Certainly.

JOHN Then forward to the Beehive.

*(*CYRIL *and* JOHN *go into the hall and start to put their coats on.)*

MR. JONES Did they give you a good lunch?

MRS. JONES Wonderful! It was served in their private suite overlooking the river. They couldn't have been nicer. Tzelnicker kissed my hand and Sokolovsky mixed me a cocktail.

JOHN Tzelnicker and Sokolovsky? Olde England United Foodstuffs Limited? But they're the people who are sponsoring this programme . . . *(He stops.)*

MRS. JONES *(prompting him)* Mrs. Jones' Journal. I know. I'm so thrilled about it.

PENNY You knew?

MRS. JONES Mrs. Benbow took me into her confidence.

CYRIL She did, did she!

PENNY When was this?

MRS. JONES Today. While we were having lunch at the Savoy. *(She rises.)*

PENNY You'd better sit down again Mother. *We* have something to tell *you.*

CYRIL Wait until you hear who's been living in this house for the past three months.

PENNY You'll never guess who Mrs. Benbow really is.

(There is a slight pause.)

MRS. JONES She's Jonathan Gabriel.

(Collapse of PENNY.*)*

PENNY *(collapsing)* No one ever tells me anything until it's common knowledge.

48

MRS. JONES *(moving to the stairs)* She'll be along later. She said she had to meet someone at the Beehive.

MISS FAIRFAX It's obviously the popular rendezvous in these parts.

PENNY You're not holding out on us are you Mother?

MRS. JONES What do you mean?

PENNY Can you tell us what last night's high jinks were all about?

MRS. JONES I can't. I wish I could. But I didn't see her. I don't even know what she looked like. *(She exits up the stairs.)*

MR. JONES She looked quite ordinary. Harmless enough.

CYRIL You weren't locked in there with her. *(He opens the main door.)*

JOHN We shan't be long.
(JOHN and CYRIL exit.)

MISS FAIRFAX Was she a burglar, do you think?

PENNY *(thoughtfully)* No . . . I don't think she was.

MR. JONES Then what was she doing here?

PENNY I think she was eavesdropping. Sitting in that chair listening to everything we were saying.

MISS FAIRFAX But why? Why should she?
(Commotion and excited voices are heard outside. CYRIL'S and JOHN'S voices are raised in triumph and another, a feminine voice, in protest.)

CYRIL *(opening the door)* In there! Go on! Inside!

THE GIRL Let go of me!

JOHN Oh no you don't. In you go!

MISS FAIRFAX Who is it?
(CYRIL and JOHN enter with the girl struggling desperately between them. She is an intense young woman of about eighteen with a very thick cold in the nose.)

CYRIL Miss Foxy-Face.

PENNY Where did you find her?

CYRIL Behind the bushes.

JOHN We mightn't have noticed her if Cyril hadn't heard her sneeze.

CYRIL I'd know that sneeze anywhere.

THE GIRL Let go of me! *(She kicks CYRIL hard on the shins.)*

CYRIL Ow ! ! !
(MRS. JONES enters at the top of the stairs.)

MRS. JONES Why whatever are you doing to Miss Bunter-Cutts?
(There is an astonished silence.)

CYRIL Is this Miss Bunter-Cutts!

MRS. JONES Of course. Do shut the door Cyril. There's a draught.

MR. JONES What were you doing inside my Guy Fawkes?

MISS BUNTER-CUTTS Well . . .

MR. JONES And while we're on the subject where are his innards?

MISS BUNTER-CUTTS I put them on the top shelf right at the back.

49

MR. JONES Do you realise this is the first time we haven't had a guy to put on our bonfire! All because of you!

MISS BUNTER-CUTTS I'm very sorry Mr. Jones.

MR. JONES You come in here . . . disembowelling other people's effigies . . . without so much as a " May I ? " . . . I've a good mind to ring up the police station and have you given in charge.

MISS BUNTER-CUTTS Please don't do that, Mr. Jones. It would start my career off on the wrong foot.

PENNY Your career?

MISS BUNTER-CUTTS Besides, the police might think Dad had put me up to it and that would spoil his record.

JOHN What record?

MISS BUNTER-CUTTS *(proudly)* Thirty years a confidential enquiry agent and never a word of censure from the Bench. Dad's very proud of that.

CYRIL A confidential . . . !

MISS BUNTER-CUTTS *(eagerly)* I've got some of Dad's cards here. *(She takes several visiting cards from her pocket and distributes them.)* I'm going to have some of my own printed when I join the firm full-time.

JOHN *(reading)* Herbert Bunter-Cutts . . . The Mask Private Investigation Agency!

MISS FAIRFAX *(reading)* Tact at all times. Discretion our watchword.

MISS BUNTER-CUTTS Dad built the firm up from a one-man business until now we employ ten operators male and female.

CYRIL A snooper! A professional snooper!

MRS. JONES So that's what he does for a living. I often wondered.

MISS BUNTER-CUTTS Dad says they've been thirty good years filled with interest. I'm following in his footsteps you see. Learning the business.

MR. JONES Ferrets. Ferrets. A whole family of ferrets.

MISS BUNTER-CUTTS *(darkly)* A private eye observes much. We learn the innermost secrets of dukes and uncover the skeletons in many a cabinet minister's closet. We see all.

MISS FAIRFAX *(returning her card)* I don't think you're very nice to know.

MISS BUNTER-CUTTS Of course it can be jolly hard work. To tell you the truth the old man's getting a bit past it. All the hanging about in damp shrubbery, shivering on hotel fire escapes . . . it's no joke at his time of life. *(She sneezes alarmingly and fumbles for her handkerchief.)*

MRS. JONES Nor at yours either. That's a very nasty cold you've got. Come along, Arabella, come and sit by the fire.

MISS BUNTER-CUTTS Thanks Mrs. Jones. *(Blowing her nose and sniffing.)* I do seem to be a bit bunged up.

MR. JONES I still want to know what she was doing inside my Guy Fawkes.

MISS BUNTER-CUTTS Well, it was all because of this Jonathan
Gabriel who writes these soppy books. *(The others exchange
glances.)* I heard Mum saying that his real identity had never
been made public and from that moment I made up my mind to
find out who he really was.

CYRIL Blow me up a gum tree.

MISS BUNTER-CUTTS It was quite a simple routine job really. I
kept a watch on the comings and goings at his publisher's office,
sorted the sheep from the goats and followed up all the likely
ones. One by one I eliminated them all. All except one. *(She
leans forward impressively.)* A woman. And where should her
trail lead but straight to this house.

JOHN Did your parents know what you were up to?

MISS BUNTER-CUTTS Oh no, I wanted it to be a surprise. I was
determined to show Dad I was a credit to him and all he'd taught
me. I wanted to prove I could handle a solo assignment.

MR. JONES Go on. What happened then?

MISS BUNTER-CUTTS Yesterday afternoon, while you were all out,
I got in through your scullery window.

CYRIL Of all the infernal cheek!

MISS BUNTER-CUTTS Then I disguised myself as the Guy Fawkes
and sat in the cupboard keeping my ears open for evidence.

CYRIL Well!

(MRS. BENBOW enters U.C. She carries a small suitcase.)

MISS FAIRFAX You've come just at the right moment.

MRS. JONES You've not met Miss Bunter-Cutts, have you.

MRS. BENBOW Not face to face. But our paths have crossed
several times in recent weeks. Her activities have been a source
of interest to me.

MISS BUNTER-CUTTS *(incredulously)* *Mine* have been to *you!*

MRS. BENBOW Ever since I realised I was being followed down
Wigmore Street.

MISS BUNTER-CUTTS Do you mean to say . . . !

MRS. BENBOW I'm an old hand at that game. *(She places the
small suitcase carefully on the large table and starts to remove her
gloves.)* During the war I was a Special Correspondent in the
Balkans. I grew eyes in the back of my head.

MISS BUNTER-CUTTS But I was so careful . . . tactful . . . unobtrusive
. . . just like Dad showed me!

MRS. BENBOW Just to make sure I led her in and out of the Wallace
Collection, twice round Spanish Place and down the steps to the
tube at Baker Street.

MISS BUNTER-CUTTS *(gloomily)* I can't think what Dad will say
when he hears about this.

MRS. BENBOW As a matter of fact, young lady, *I've* been having
you followed.

JISS BUNTER-CUTTS Oh no!

MRS. BENBOW Since you were taking such an interest in me it seemed only courteous to return the compliment. *(She glances at her watch)* Chambers should be here at any moment.

JOHN Chambers?

PENNY Who's Chambers?

MRS. BENBOW Better known officially as Detective Sergeant Nancy Chambers . . . " Chambers of the Yard."

(The doorbell rings.)

MISS BUNTER-CUTTS Nancy Chambers . . . !

MR. JONES That'll teach you to come snooping about my house.

MISS FAIRFAX The snooper snooped.

(PENNY opens the door.)

MRS. BENBOW Come in Sergeant. *(MISS CHAMBERS enters.)* I've just told them who you are.

MISS CHAMBERS You've got her I see.

MISS BUNTER-CUTTS *(excitedly)* Sergeant Nancy Chambers of the Peacehaven Beach Hut Case?

MISS CHAMBERS *(grimly)* The same.

MISS BUNTER-CUTTS And Lord Lamport and the Girl Guides?

MISS CHAMBERS Correct.

MISS BUNTER-CUTTS Wasn't it you who rounded up the Jermyn Street Gang?

MISS CHAMBERS On the strength of my evidence they got fifteen years apiece.

MRS. BENBOW *(unwrapping bottles from the suitcase at the table)* You may also remember Sergeant Chambers in connection with the Peckham White Slavers, the Battersea Bigamist and numerous other Sunday paper sensations.

CYRIL Crikey! *(He regards MISS CHAMBERS with awe.)*

MISS CHAMBERS I've had a talk with the Station Sergeant. If you care to give the word we'll make out a warrant for her arrest. Unlawful entry, trespass, wilful damage, housebreaking, loitering with intent to commit a felony . . . .

MISS BUNTER-CUTTS *(horrified)* You're not talking about me . . .?

(MRS. BENBOW moves to the sideboard and starts to pour out drinks.)

MRS. JONES I don't think that will be necessary, Mrs. Benbow. I'd be obliged if you could just let the matter rest.

MRS. BENBOW As you wish. Is that all right with you, Nancy?

MISS CHAMBERS It's entirely up to you.

MRS. BENBOW Then the case is closed. It seems a shame after all the work you've put in.

MISS CHAMBERS That' all right. You've done me many a favour. I'm glad to have been of some small service in return.

MISS BUNTER-CUTTS *(her eyes shining with hero worship)* It's such a thrill actually meeting you. I've always wanted to . . . ever since I read your revelations in the " Evening Post " " Secrets of a Lady Sleuth."

MISS CHAMBERS *(sternly)* Now you listen to me. As far as you're concerned this lady is still Mrs. Benbow. Not a word to your parents about Jonathan Gabriel or I'll have you inside quicker than you can say Jack the Ripper. Is that understood?

MISS BUNTER-CUTTS *(breathless with adoration)* Oh yes Ma'am. I'll do anything you say. Could I . . . could I please have your autograph? *(She offers* MISS CHAMBERS *a soiled envelope and a ball-point pen.)*

MRS. BENBOW You're a very lucky young woman. It's thanks to Sergeant Chambers that you didn't spend last night in the cells.

MR. JONES How was that?

MISS CHAMBERS *(autographing the back of the envelope)* If I hadn't switched off the lights . . .

JOHN It was you!

MISS CHAMBERS We knew where to find her when we were ready.

MRS. BENBOW We didn't want this particular balloon to go up until the other business was settled.
(Having filled glasses for all she now, with JOHN'S *assistance, hands them round.)*

MISS CHAMBERS If you want to be a *real* detective you take my advice and join the Force. It's as well to have the Law on your side. *(She returns the envelope and pen.)*

MISS BUNTER-CUTTS Oh, thank you! I shall always remember this evening.

JOHN *(chuckling)* You're not the only one.

MRS. BENBOW Now then . . . I want you all to try some of this vodka.

CYRIL Vodka!

MISS FAIRFAX Where did you get this from? The Beehive?

MRS. BENBOW No. I collected it this evening from the Jugoslav Embassy. A personal present from Marshal Tito's own cellar.

CYRIL I'm beginning to wonder who you *really* are!

MRS. BENBOW Shall we say . . . just a " a stranger in the house." Here's to the success of all our enterprises.

MRS. JONES Here's to you, Reg. This is your moment of triumph. You've waited a long time for it.

MRS. BENBOW Ah, Mrs. Jones. You are a woman of rare understanding . . . the rock on which this household rests. I count it a privilege to have known you. Your husband is a fortunate man.

MR. JONES I'm inclined to agree with you. *(He puts an arm around his wife's shoulders.)*

JOHN *(raising his glass)* To the Jones family! Success to the journal!

ALL *(except* BUNTER-CUTTS *and* CHAMBERS*)* Success to the journal!
FROM THIS POINT THE SCENE IS PLAYED VERY QUICKLY UNTIL ONLY JOHN AND PENNY REMAIN.

CYRIL Three cheers for the THING!

ALL *(except* BUNTER-CUTTS *and* CHAMBERS*)* Hip . . . hip . . .
Hurrah!

MR. JONES And now let's light the bonfire. *(He struggles into
his coat assisted by* MISS CHAMBERS.*)*

MISS FAIRFAX *(lifting the lid of the cardboard box)* Flaming
Dragons . . Fiery Whizzbangs . . ! What a time you're going
to have!

CYRIL *(picking up the box and extending his free hand to* MISS
FAIRFAX*)* Come on . . let's make the sparks fly!
*(*CYRIL *and* MISS FAIRFAX *exit through the windows U.R. into the
garden.)*

JOHN *(to* MR. JONES*)* I think you must be the oldest schoolboy
in England.

MRS. BENBOW *(moving to the windows)* Will you join us, Nancy?

MISS CHAMBERS *(laughing)* By all means. *(She crosses to the
windows.)*

MRS. BENBOW We're all pagans under the skin.
*(*MRS. BENBOW *and* MISS CHAMBERS *exit into the garden.)*

MRS. JONES I'll stay here and keep Arabella company. She won't
want to go out into the garden. Not with that nasty cold.

MISS BUNTER-CUTTS Oh but I'd love to let off a flaming dragon.
If you could spare one.

MR. JONES *(breathing hard)* Yes, all right then. Come along.

MISS BUNTER-CUTTS I'm having a lovely time. We never had any
fireworks at our house. Can I come again next year?

MR. JONES *(under his breath)* What a family! Here . . sit in this.
(He indicates the wheelchair.)

MISS BUNTER-CUTTS Me? What for?

MR. JONES Don't argue. Do as you're told. *(*MRS. JONES
switches off the standard lamp as MISS BUNTER-CUTTS *quickly sits
in the wheelcair.)*

MR. JONES *(wheeling* MISS BUNTER-CUTTS *to the window)* I've got
a damn good idea.

MRS. JONES *(preceding them to hold the windows wide)* Have you
Reg? What is it?

MR. JONES *(as they exit)* Suppose we put her on the bonfire?
*(*MRS. JONES *laughs and* MISS BUNTER-CUTTS *half rises in alarm
as she is wheeled off.* PENNY, *throughout the business of the
general exodus, has remained motionless, her eyes on* JOHN.
JOHN, *at the window, now looks across the empty stage at* PENNY.*)*

CYRIL *(calling from off right)* Come on, you two. Hurry up!
We're just going to light the bonfire!
*(*PENNY *moves R.C. and turns off the main lights. When the lights
have gone out, but not before,* CYRIL'S *voice is heard again distant.*

CYRIL What's going on in there?
*(*JOHN *moves to* PENNY *and takes her in his arms.)*

JOHN *(softly)* Poor Penny.

PENNY *(in a whisper)* Dear John.

(He holds her in silence for a second.)
JOHN   I'm glad you're not an enigmatic slinky type.
PENNY *(sadly)*   Are you? Why?
JOHN   This business of love at first sight . . .   *(He stops.)*
PENNY   Yes?
JOHN   The odd thing is . . . I find it works both ways.
PENNY *(ecstatically happy she lifts her face to his)*   Oh . . . John!
   Darling!
   *(They kiss. There is a series of loud explosions from the garden
   . . . a pandemonium of Whistling Whizzbangs, Jumping Devil-
   Crackers, etc., accompanied by excited voices, flickering flames
   and coloured firework effects.)*
   *(PENNY and JOHN take no notice whatever and hold their kiss
   as . . .)*

THE CURTAIN FALLS

PROPERTY LIST

ACT ONE
On stage

White sheet over the " Thing."

Two cushions each in the upstage and the downstage armchairs.

Key to cupboard. Hanging on hook beside cupboard door.

CYRIL'S and MR. JONES' overcoats with gloves in pockets, scarves and hats, clothes brush. On coat stand.

Pen and papers on writing desk.

Sundry small pieces of wire and metal, box of matches in ashtray, two empty coffee cups in saucers. On small table before fire.

Small first aid box, book with gay cover bearing the title " Love Among The Scented Blossoms," bottle of whisky, six small glasses. On top of sideboard.

CYRIL'S wristwatch. On mantelpiece.

MRS. BENBOW's briefcase containing a large fat envelope. By the right side of the upstage armchair.

Book in upstage armchair.

Off left

Several small bottles of nail varnish. (PENNY).

Newspaper (PENNY).

Shoe cleaning materials (CYRIL).

Newspaper (CYRIL).

Pair of well polished shoes (MR. JONES).

Screwdriver (MR. JONES).

Off right

Pair of shoes (CYRIL).

Torch (MISS CHAMBERS).

Personal

MRS. BENBOW Cheroot. Briefcase key in coat pocket.

CYRIL Handkerchief. Cigarette.

PENNY Wristwatch.

ACT TWO
On stage

Evening newspaper, open at crossword puzzle. On small table before fire.

CYRIL'S overcoat with full packet of cigarettes in pocket, scarf, gloves and hat. On coat stand.

Check matches still in ashtray, whisky and glasses still on sideboard, cupboard key still on hook.

Off left

Coffee percolator (JOHN).

Small frilly plastic apron (JOHN).

Tray containg two cups and saucers, milk jug and sugar bowl (PENNY).

Another smaller tray containing two cups and saucers and a small plate of cakes (PENNY).

Packet of cigars (MRS. BENBOW).

Personal

CYRIL Pencil. Sheet of notepaper with writing on it. Cigarette case containing only a few cigarettes. Cigarette lighter.

JOHN Wristwatch.

MISS FAIRFAX Wristwatch.

ACT THREE
On stage

CYRIL'S and MR. JONES' overcoats. On coat stand.

Six fresh glasses. On sideboard.

Check copy of " Love Among The Scented Blossoms " still on sideboard.

Off left

Copy of " Radio Times " (PENNY).

Cardboard box containing a few prop fireworks (MR. JONES).

Six empty bottles with stick rockets protruding from them (MR. JONES).

Off right

Small suitcase in which are two bottles containing water (supposedly vodka) (MRS. BENBOW).

Personal

MRS. JONES Cheque in handbag.

ARABELLA Several visiting cards. Handkerchief. Soiled envelope. Ball point pen.

MRS. BENBOW Wristwatch.